To Ethan,

May your favourite Sports team bring you joy!

Sid Greneman
Jan. 20, 2018

ISBN 978-0-692-90752-8

Seabird Press

Cover art and page layout: Lisa Daly

America's Sports Fans and Their Teams:

WHO ROOTS FOR WHOM AND WHY

by Sid Groeneman

This book is dedicated to the memory of Ron Wise,
a passionate sports fan and true mensch,
who enriched the lives of everyone
who had the good fortune
of knowing him.

Table of Contents

Preface

I'm a sports fan, and you probably are too. This is a book for sports fans. It's full of numbers—but not the usual stats about players or teams. This book is about YOU— the fan. If you want to know how players or teams measure up using conventional indicators, there are many easy-to-access sources you may consult. If you want to be introduced to new ideas in sports statistics, read Bill James or Nate Silver. But if you are interested in sports FANS, then this is your book.

America's Sports Fans and Their Teams: Who Roots for Whom and Why examines why fans like to watch sporting events and follow certain teams. It looks at who America's sports fans are, which sports they like to watch, which teams they like to follow, and attempts to explain why. It describes how fans differ from those who don't follow sports, and how fans of different sports are alike and dissimilar. The book also presents national popularity rankings of all teams in Major League Baseball, the National Football League, the National Basketball Association, and the National Hockey League.

Perhaps most ambitiously, it presents uniquely detailed inventories and rankings of reasons why fans like their favorite professional team sport and favorite team, and why they chose to follow that team. Beyond the numbers, it illustrates those reasons with quotations from sports enthusiasts throughout the country, capturing the fascinating diversity that makes up America's fans.

The research for this book required more than scrupulous fact-checking. As a survey specialist by trade, I planned and carried out the primary research through a large-scale national survey coupled with 80 in-depth personal interviews.

While conducting the background search of existing sources, I found nothing quite like it that answers the question "Who roots for whom and why?" The book should be of interest to sophisticated sports enthusiasts curious about what motivates fans. The information and analysis should have special utility for sports marketing professionals, sportswriters, and students of fandom.

• • •

America's Sports Fans and Their Teams: Who Roots for Whom and Why is based on original research. The presentation expands upon and enhances the insights in prior writing by sportswriters, essayists, and academics, as well as benefits from their work.

Acknowledgements

I am indebted to many for their wisdom, expertise, and encouragement during the two years it took to develop the research and prepare the manuscript. The staff at Soapbox, a division of Interviewing Services of America in Los Angeles, who assisted with the survey implementation, merit a special call out. So do the dedicated tech support people at SurveyGizmo.com in Boulder, Colorado, who provided the survey platform and helped with the programming. My research would have been immeasurably harder without their expertise and responsive service.

This book also benefitted from the considerable talent of my editing and production team, including Alison DeLuca (team leader), Lisa Daly of GoodCo Graphics (cover design and page layout), Audrey Hoisinger (copy editing), and Jake Palmer (e-book formatting). Apart from their expert professional assistance, they were a joy to work with.

Four friends reviewed chapter drafts and provided invaluable advice. Michael Denomme, author of *How to Quote Shakespeare in Everyday Life*, offered ongoing support throughout the project and taught me important things that a first-time author needs to know. Steve Grant, author of *The Russian Nanny: Real and Imagined*, was a meticulous early version editor and font of creative suggestions. Larry Bruser, a serious and truly knowledgeable sports fan, provided critical feedback that steered me in the right direction, as did Danny Aharoni. Another friend, Alan Roshwalb—a statistician and former co-worker—calculated the weights for the survey data. All five contributed significantly. Any omissions, errors in analysis or interpretation, ambiguities of presentation, and other flaws in the final product are on me.

My son Michael deserves a shout-out for recruiting subjects to help test the in-depth-interview questions and by adding his approval to the Chapter 1 draft. Above all, my wife, Beth Groeneman, who did a first-run edit of each chapter draft and was consistently supportive of the time (and other resources) spent on the project, when I might have been engaged in more mutually beneficial activities. I cannot thank her enough.

Sid Groeneman
Bethesda, Maryland
August, 2017

Chapter 1:

Sports Fans, Sports Followed, and Team Allegiances

Sports is, somehow, a religion. You either see
or you don't see what the excitement is.
– Michael Novak, *The Joy of Sports*

It's a question that's long puzzled sports journalists and commentators, marketing professionals, and even some academics: Why do fans become attached to one team over another, especially when they reject their local or hometown option? This mystery, in turn, begs two prior questions: Who become sports fans in the first place, and which sports are they attracted to? You would think that an individual must be interested in a sport before developing an allegiance to a particular team, but the opposite is also possible.

While most would agree that rooting for your preferred team enhances the spectator experience, it is not uncommon to watch a game without being partial to one side or the other. You can enjoy watching sports without having a favorite team to root for through appreciation of the sheer athleticism on display or by savoring the intense competition between closely matched opponents or long-time rivals.

My own interest in sports and favorite teams began when I was young. Some of my sharpest (and fondest) memories are of playing sports almost daily in my 1950s working-class neighborhood in Toledo, Ohio. Toledo was, and is, a medium-size city fueled by its auto parts manufacturing, vehicle assembly, and glass industries. Known best for two highly regarded attractions—its art museum and zoo[1]—Toledo had not yet begun its decline as part of the country's rust belt.

Depending on the season and the weather, my friends and I would gather to play football on the grassy field across the street from where I lived, or for softball and basketball on the asphalt playground next to my elementary school. These were pick-up games, often played three on three or two on two—a far cry from organized full-team competition—but great fun despite, or perhaps because of, the informality. I was fortunate that my neighborhood was filled with other kids about my age. Easy accessibility was also key—we could be out of the house and playing ball at a moment's notice. This was before large-scale suburbanization, when it became more commonplace for parents to have to shuttle kids around at pre-arranged times to play ball outdoors.

I was eight or nine years old when my interest in following professional sports teams sprouted. In my case, there wasn't an easy or obvious "home team" choice. Although Toledo has been the home of the fabled triple-A baseball Mud Hens for over 100 years, as well as a series of minor league hockey teams, the city was not large enough to support its own major league franchise.

However, Toledo is situated between Detroit (60 miles north) and Cleveland (120 miles east), each offering a choice of Major League Baseball teams and National Football League teams to root for. In addition, Detroit had the basketball Pistons and the hockey Red Wings, as they still do, and Cleveland currently hosts the Cavaliers basketball team.

Apart from Toledo sports fans' major professional league choices—the Tigers or Indians (in baseball), and the Lions or Browns (in the NFL)—residents of the area have also been divided along the Ann Arbor/Columbus axis in college athletics. I'm referring, of course, to the iconic rivalry between the University of Michigan Wolverines and the Ohio State Buckeyes. Toledo sports fans intensely identify with one school or the other. A t-shirt popular among Buckeye fans reads: *My favorite teams are Ohio State and whoever is playing Michigan*. Wolverine fans prefer the shirt that reads: *A buckeye is some kind of nut*.

A friend and high school classmate who graduated from Ohio State went so far as to paint his house scarlet and grey (Ohio State's colors) and name his son "Jacob Woody," after the Buckeyes' legendary football coach Woody Hayes. Because I'd attended Michigan, our friendship was precarious—and at times contentious.

The Buckeye Wolverine Shop was located on Monroe Street in the Toledo suburb of Sylvania, a short distance from the state line and the entrance ramp to U.S. Route 23 heading north toward Ann Arbor.[2] Ohio State and Michigan fans could purchase collectibles and accessories conforming to their allegiance on either the left side or right side of the store, sharply demarcated by a broad stripe running down the center of the floor. Over the years, much has been written about the long and bitter Ohio State - Michigan rivalry, which is another reason Toledo is an epicenter of heated competition for fan loyalties. One might think that relative distance to Detroit/Cleveland (or Ann Arbor/Columbus) matters most. However, Cleveland's (and Columbus's) in-state status at least partly counter-balances any proximity advantage for the Michigan teams. (Be sure to read the Afterword.)

So, how does a budding young baseball or football fan acquire a favorite team when there are no local teams, but pairs of competing choices nearby?

A personal odyssey

As mentioned, I began looking for an answer to this enigma by reflecting on how my own sports interests and team loyalties developed. In baseball, I became a strong Cleveland Indians fan around the age of nine. I don't recall having had any abiding spectator sports interests before that time, although I do remember entertaining sympathies for Ohio State teams (before I knew better!) due to naïve home state chauvinism. I recall cheering on OSU's powerhouse basketball teams featuring Jerry Lucas, John Havlicek, and Bobby Knight. My allegiance to the Cleveland Browns, inspired by Hall-of-Fame running back Jim Brown, also began at about age 9. Nearer to home, the University of Toledo Rockets also captured my attention.

Neither of my parents were sports fans. Both were immigrants, born in Eastern Europe, who had difficulty appreciating American sports culture. I had no brothers or sisters, so influence of immediate family does not explain my sports fan interests. I did have a cousin close to my age living down the street. His love of golf piqued my interest in the game. It wasn't long before I became a fan of Arnold Palmer who, along with Gary Player and Jack Nicklaus, were the PGA tour's premier players at the time.

As for professional team sports, it was the Cleveland Indians that attracted my greatest attention. Thinking back, I probably chose the Indians as my favorite baseball team because they were the closest in-state major league team—the home state loyalist that I was. But there was another important influence: my next-door neighbor Harold, a cab driver and staunch Indians fan, who would listen to games in his rocking chair on the front porch. Harold had two daughters including one my age. But at nine years old, I was much more interested in sports than girls.

Sitting on the porch with Harold listening to Indians games and discussing baseball remain some of my most vivid memories. Had it not been for him, I might not have developed an interest in the Cleveland Indians—at least not as early or as intensely. It didn't hurt that the Indians had an exciting team with players like slugger Rocky Colavito, nor that they were in the thick of the American League pennant race late into the 1959 season. It was the first year I remember following them, and I remember my devastation when they ultimately lost out to the Chicago White Sox.

My sports team loyalties didn't change much during my high school and college years, although I do remember developing an interest in the Los Angeles Lakers in basketball. Initially, I was a fan of Laker standouts Jerry West and Wilt Chamberlain, and later, Kareem Abdul-Jabbar and Magic Johnson. After leaving Toledo at 17 to attend the University of Michigan, I naturally became a huge fan of Wolverines sports.

Despite living in Detroit for two years after graduating, my favorites remained the Indians in baseball and the Browns in professional football. I remained exclusively a Browns fan until I moved to Minneapolis to attend graduate school in the 1970s, at which time I starting rooting for the Minnesota Vikings. That allegiance continued until I moved to the Washington DC area in 1980 to start my first regular full-time job as a study director for a company that does surveys and marketing research. I tried rooting for the home-team Redskins, who were enjoying considerable success at the time, but the relentless Redskins media hype eventually turned me off. If that hadn't pushed me away, Dan Snyder, who later became the team's controversial owner, surely would have. Since then, I've become a fair-weather fan of the Baltimore Ravens, although I've mostly lost interest in watching NFL games.

I continue to follow basketball, watching the local Washington Wizards in the NBA and rooting for the University of Maryland Terrapins at the college level, situated in nearby College Park (as well as the Wolverines). I never became much of a hockey fan, although I do tune in to an occasional Pittsburgh Penguins game when they are on TV—but mainly because I have a life-long affection for penguins (and penguin team logos), rather than because I have any special interest in hockey or the city of Pittsburgh.

From the start, my number one spectator sport has been baseball. Looking back, this might be due largely to having played little league baseball for four years and to my signature lifetime sports achievement at the age of twelve—helping my school team, the Cherry Stars, reach the finals in the 1962 city of Toledo championship tournament.[3]

Not until much later, when I moved to Minneapolis in 1973, did my baseball loyalty shift from the Cleveland Indians to the Minnesota Twins. Nevertheless, I still have a soft spot in my heart—and probably always will have—for the Indians (and also the Browns) because of where I grew up and because of my natural inclination to favor teams from underdog cities. My interest in the Twins originated from a desire to support my new city and region, which I loved, and was reinforced by watching all-star second baseman Rod Carew, my favorite player. I later spent a year in northern New Jersey and flirted briefly with the Mets, but that interest never took hold, perhaps because they weren't very good at the time.

When I moved to Washington, it didn't take long to become strongly attached to the successful Baltimore Orioles, then the closest Major League Baseball team. My family and I loved making the occasional 40-mile trek north on I-95 to watch the Orioles play, first at the old Memorial Stadium and, since 1992, at their beautiful Camden Yards ballpark.

As the Orioles' fortunes began to fade, I switched once again, this time to the newly arrived Washington Nationals. Another reason was my opposition to O's owner Peter Angelos, who became increasingly aggressive in trying to prevent Washington from acquiring a major league team (although ultimately failing). Since 2005, my wife and I have become passionate Nats fans.

Variety and commonality in sports interests and team preferences

My personal story illustrates a variety of factors that might account for how and why team allegiances originate and change. It depicts how one young sports enthusiast, growing up in a city lacking hometown choices, settled on his favorites and later shifted. It suggests that while geographic proximity might be the number one factor accounting for team preferences, it is surely not the only one, and in some cases, not the dominant factor.

Like those in Toledo, many sports fans live in places other than major metropolitan regions with professional franchises. For them, factors other than hometown preference must come into play. Additionally, some large population centers have multiple teams for fans to choose from—places like Chicago, southern California, northern California, and, of course, New York City. Fans' choices warrant analysis to determine if common patterns exist, which might yield a general interpretation of team preference and help us better understand the process of developing and maintaining interest in a favorite team.

Emphasizing the above types of locations is not meant to imply that fans who reside in Milwaukee, Miami, Phoenix, or other areas with a single, home-team choice in football, baseball, or other professional sports always select or stick with their local option. Later sections of the book document that non-home team loyalties are more prevalent than some might imagine. When it comes to who roots for whom, we'll learn that geography is far from the whole story.

Even if proximity or the "hometown effect" does prove to be the dominant reason for fans' favorite team, it should still be interesting to investigate how often prior allegiances are maintained, especially following residential relocation, and how often the new local team preferences prevail. America has a highly mobile population. Exactly what does it take for local teams in a sports fan's new location to dislodge existing loyalties? Are allegiances perhaps stronger or more enduring for those who live (or grew up) in smaller communities with less competition for fan loyalties or with fewer leisure time options in general?

In conducting the research for this book, I encountered sports fans who lived in the same area their entire life and never considered shifting their allegiance, and others whose loyalties faded due to lack of team success or other reasons. I also talked with fans who moved but never renounced their original hometown preference, and still others who, like me, moved multiple times and adopted new local favorites with successive moves. Apart from these variations, I also identified fans whose favorite team was entirely unrelated to where they live or used to live.

My research also identifies numerous reasons why a sport or team interest originates or solidifies including, among others: (a) early childhood family experiences (watching football on TV with a beloved grandparent); (b) being a source of spousal or family bonding (a reason mentioned disproportionately by female fans); (c) identification with a gritty blue-collar city filled with fans who don't give up (as in Cleveland or Pittsburgh); (d) positive civic impacts that a team provides (such as the pride inspired by arrival of the Oklahoma City Thunder in a region which had never had a major team franchise, or the New Orleans Saints' contributions to the city after Hurricane Katrina); (e) ethnic pride (of a Los Angeles Latino whose loyalty to the Dodgers was cemented by the emergence of pitcher Fernando Valenzuela); (f) fascination with the game's physicality (mentioned by many football and hockey fans); and (g) the basic human need to have some team to root for (mentioned by a fan of the San Diego Chargers). My research also revealed idiosyncratic circumstances or chance events—one example being the case of a young African-American male who became a diehard New York Knicks fan after getting a free ticket to a game at Madison Square Garden from his high school teacher. Subsequent sections illustrate these and other motivations.

Although virtually all fan histories have some unique qualities—which add variety and interest—I will focus mostly on the commonalities and highlight the prevalent patterns.

Objectives and game plan

My purpose in writing this book is to bring hard evidence to bear on a few broad questions:

(1) How many sports fans are there (based on a carefully formulated definition of "sports fan")? Do fans differ from non-fans? How are fans of different sports similar

and different from one another? Are professional basketball fans demographically much the same as baseball fans? Are hockey fans more fanatical than football fans? These questions enable testing common presuppositions and stereotypes, focusing in particular on fans of the four major professional team sports in the U.S. ("big4"). Chapter 2 begins by describing the concept of "sports fan" used in this book and estimates how many fans there are in each sport and overall. Chapter 3 profiles fans of different sports, noting similarities and contrasts.

(2) What theories can be applied to help understand team allegiances? Chapter 4 outlines three general models that have been used to account for people's attachments (as viewers and followers) to sports and teams. The underlying ideas overlap as much as they compete with one another for validity and utility.

(3) Why do fans like watching their favorite professional team sport? What attracts some fans more to the NBA more than to the NFL, for example? Is it because they played that sport when young? Because of family or friends? Because it's accessible? A myriad of reasons are plausible. While no single explanation will apply in all cases, Chapter 5 will investigate whether some reasons predominate and if patterns emerge depending on the sport.

(4) What are U.S. sports fans' favorite teams, and why do they like being fans? Chapter 6 ranks the big4 teams by the number of fans nationally who select them as their favorite team to watch and follow, and speculates why some are more popular than their "natural" (geographic) fan base would suggest.

(5) What is it that fans like about their overall favorite team, and how did that initial attachment originate? Chapters 7 and 8 analyze these factors to help uncover what qualities, beliefs, values, and practices are important in generating and sustaining team attachments.

(6) What percentage of fans have switched from one favorite team to another during their lifetime? Chapter 9 estimates how many fans have ever switched to their current favorite from a different one in the same sport and examines the main reasons why.

(7) The concluding section (chapter 10) recaps the main take-aways from the analysis and speculates about the future of sports fandom.

While I concentrate on presenting the numbers from my Sports Fan Survey (in keeping with the intent of addressing the objectives using fresh statistical research),

I illustrate the general patterns, as well as the interesting exceptions, with quotations and a few more extended stories from the fans themselves to make the numbers "come alive" and introduce the fascinating diversity which characterizes America's sports fans.

Data and research procedures

My intent is to move beyond anecdotes and impressions to address the above questions systematically. This implies having the requisite data, which is only achievable through primary research. While there might be fragments of publicly available information relevant to some of these questions (my search did not turn up much—and virtually nothing permitting careful quantification), there is no single source or combination of sources that remotely addresses all of these issues.

So, to fill this gap and provide fresh data for this book, I developed and conducted a national survey of sports fans. Because surveys have been my lifetime work—having designed, conducted, analyzed, and reported on over 200 of them covering a broad range of topics over a 35-year career—this was second nature for me, although, as always, challenging to do well.

The survey, conducted online, was completed by 1,825 adults from across the country—1,303 of whom qualified to complete the full survey, and 522 who were not fans of any "big 4" professional team sports and were not administered the full series of questions.[4] The survey was conducted in two periods—during the fall (2015) and the spring (2016)—to balance out possible seasonal effects in the way people think and talk about their spectator sports interests and practices.

Beyond the 1,825 responses to the survey, which enables estimation of fan populations and the other statistics used in the book, I also personally conducted 80 follow-up telephone interviews with selected survey respondents to obtain more in-depth, qualitative information to add color and provide real-life examples of the statistical patterns uncovered in the survey.

A more detailed account of the methodology appears in the appendix.

We begin in the next chapter by presenting estimates of the various sports fan populations and examine how sports fans differ from non-fans.

Chapter 2:

Sports Fandom, Fan Estimates, Dominance of the NFL

*Ultimately sports is one of the deepest and most
profound expressions of culture that we have.*
– Eric Simons, *The Secret Lives of Sports Fans*

Scope and impact

Spectator sports are an overwhelmingly consequential part of American life and popular culture. Fans devote countless hours following sports and spend billions each year on ticket purchases, television and internet subscriptions, team paraphernalia, books, magazines, and newspapers indulging our appetite to follow sports and to support our favorite teams.[5] The teams that excel become the stuff of legend, as do the most exceptional players, who become our heroes. While it is impossible to fully capture the role sports play for fans, it is hard to imagine life without it.

In addition to providing stimulating, sometimes riveting, entertainment or simply a relaxed way of filling time, sports have more serious impacts, such as providing social benefits. For one, spectator sports can be an integrative force, helping build community and harmonize diverse elements in society. It can serve as a source of civic pride and, in some cases, accelerate the revitalization of declining neighborhoods, as with the construction of Pacific Bell Park (now AT&T Park) in San Francisco in 2000.[6] It is said that the one thing Democrats and Republicans in my own community can agree upon is the success of the Washington Redskins.

James Stibbs, a spokesman for Britain's Sport and Recreation Alliance, in lamenting the November 2015 terrorist attack at the Paris soccer stadium Stade de France, calls sports "… one of the best tools we have for bridging differences."[7] Particularly in America, where the sources of social cleavage are numerous, team sports can be a source of integration … and can promote social solidarity.[8] Because sport is often enjoyed in groups, it has the capacity to connect people who wouldn't otherwise come together.[9] As Mark, a 32 year-old Marylander and fan of the Baltimore Ravens expressed it, "rooting for a team provides something in common with others and unites people of different backgrounds."

Watching sports can provide an outlet for emotional expression and diminish feelings of apathy, marginalization, or neglect. Others point to sports' role in socialization, as in conveying positive values to young people—the values which civil society requires. Some contend that it can help build social capital, and can even become a component of collective identity, as hockey has in Canada.[10] For other fans, sports spectating may simply be a way of indulging in nostalgic memories of childhood experiences.

Literary editor and essayist Joseph Epstein relates a personal story illustrating how a common sports interest can have power to transcend social class and education:

> Some years ago I found myself working in the South among men with whom I shared nothing in the way or region, religion, education, politics, or general views; we shared nothing, in fact, but sports, which was enough for us to get along and grow to become friends, along the way showing how superficial all the things that might have kept us apart in fact were.[11]

Sports fandom can also have less positive societal impacts, as when it deteriorates into rowdy or boorish behavior, drunkenness, divisive chauvinism, or worse—violent hooliganism, which, fortunately for us in America, is more pronounced in Europe.

For others, being a sports fan carries negative connotations of passivity (being a "couch potato") or avoidance of more intellectual or productive pursuits. Among non-fans, writes Joe Queenan, "there seems to be a general feeling that following sports is a colossal waste of time."[12] Writer-humorist Fran Lebowitz once commented, only partly tongue in cheek, how sad it is for the human race that so many smart people are interested in sports.[13] While not always expressed as bluntly, for Lebowitz as for others, "[Sports fans'] intense preoccupation with men performing odd, combative group exercises all centered on a mere ball seems unaccountable."[14]

As philosopher and writer Michael Novak suggests, such sentiments smack of highbrow elitism, observing how sports fans are looked down upon by intellectuals (and those aspiring to be), and has become associated with being lower class, adolescent, and patriotic. In his contrary perspective, "The basic reality of all human life is play, games, sport; these are the realities from which the basic metaphors for all that is important in the rest of life are drawn."[15]

It is far from my purpose to argue whether sports spectating has, on net, more positive or negative societal consequences—only to note in passing that it surely produces both types and sometimes conjures stereotypes. More to the point is offering some fresh statistics, which suggest the depth and breadth of its penetration and highlight its prominence.

Who's a "sports fan"?

Some researchers distinguish between spectators and fans, arguing either that not all spectators are fans—meaning spectators can be casual, detached viewers of a sporting event and not particularly engaged, or that spectating implies watching sports events in person, and fans can't always watch games in person. Others say being a fan means being a devotee of the game, having familiarity with the contestants and a deep understanding of the rules and norms of the game, while a spectator is not necessarily as knowledgeable.[16]

While I readily admit that not all spectators are fans, these issues, which might be relevant in academic research, are oblique to my objectives. I use "spectator" and "fan" interchangeably, with the understanding that being a spectator implies being a fan and vice versa. Nevertheless, clarity of presentation requires unambiguous use of the term "sports fan". I use two definitions of differing breadth in this book, the choice of which will depend on the specific topic being addressed.

(1) My narrower definition of sports fan—the one that will be used most—refers to someone who watches and follows at least one of the four main U.S. professional team sports (NFL football, Major League Baseball, NBA basketball, and/or NHL hockey. For brevity, they are hereafter referred to as the "big4"). Unless otherwise noted, "sports fan" refers to this population.

While I recognize that "sports fan" generally implies a broader universe in everyday conversation, I focus on big4 sports leagues, especially beyond this chapter, because they raise the least predictable and therefore most interesting issues of team allegiance. My focus on the big4 is by no means meant to imply the illegitimacy of considering as sports fans those who enjoy watching individual or non-professional team sports, professional sports played at lower levels, or team sports played primarily in other countries (like soccer).

(2) My second, broader definition expands the notion of "sports fan" to encompass, in addition to fans of one or more of the big4, those who watch and follow team and non team sports played professionally besides the big4 or at the college level (NCAA – all divisions).[17] I use this broader definition less often, primarily in this chapter and the next, to estimate their respective numbers and compare them to big4 fans. As will be evident below, there are relatively few definition 2 fans who are not also definition 1 fans.

One key feature of both definitions bears noting: "Watch and follow" is explicitly intended to exclude the casual spectator who might occasionally watch a game, or

Table 2.1: Sports Fan Populations
Estimates based on 248 million U.S. persons 18 and older
(Percentages are rounded to the nearest whole percent; population estimates are rounded to the nearest million.)

Sport	% of U.S. Adults	U.S. Adult Population (millions)	Ranking
NFL football	62%	154	1
MLB baseball	41%	102	2
NBA basketball	36%	89	3
NHL hockey	22%	54	6
Fan of any "big4" professional team sport (def 1)	72%	177	
College football	34%	85	4
College basketball	26%	64	5
Auto racing	21%	51	7
Professional golf	17%	42	8
Professional tennis	14%	34	9
Professional soccer	11%	27	10
Other professional or college sports	6%	15	
Fan of *any* college or professional sport (def 2)	77%	192	

simply be in the room when a game is being telecast, but has no abiding interest in the sport.

We now turn to data from my 2015-16 Sports Fan Survey to estimate how many sports fans there are in the United States and how many fans each sport commands.

Approximately three-quarters of U.S. adults follow some sport; NFL is number 1

Most of us—77% of U.S. adults (192 million)—follow some sport at the college or professional level (our broader concept of "sports fan"); 23% (57 million adults) report no interest. Seventy-two percent (177 million adults) follow at least one big4 sport. Among fans of any sport at the college or professional level (the population encompassed by the broader definition 2), an overwhelming proportion (177M/192M=92%) watch and follow at least one of the big4 professional team sports.

Professional (NFL) football is by far the leading spectator sport in the United States. Nearly 5 of every 8 adults—154 million people—report watching and following NFL football. Major League Baseball is a distant second, with 102 million fans (41% of adults). NBA basketball ranks third, with 89 million fans. College football, college basketball, and NHL hockey follow in order. Estimates for these and other commonly followed sports are shown in the Table 2.1.

Of course, these figures do not equate to live attendance at games, which is contingent upon many factors, not the least of which are the number of games and facility capacity. By this very imperfect, alternative measure of popularity, Major League Baseball leads by a wide margin due to its much longer regular season schedule. Furthermore, compared to basketball and hockey facilities, baseball stadiums have far larger capacity.[18]

A better, but still flawed, measure of popularity, which returns NFL football to its number 1 position, is total annual revenue generated. Although the data are a few years old, NFL revenues exceed those of the three others in the big4 despite football's shorter season. Total NFL revenues are estimated to be $9.2 billion, compared to $7.1B for Major League Baseball, $4.6B for the NBA, and $2.6B for the NHL.[19] The major source of income is television contracts, which pay the NFL about $5 billion annually, compared to $1.5B for baseball and just under $1B for professional basketball.

Characteristics of Fans and Non-Fans

Men are more likely to be sports fans; other contrasts are mostly minor.

By a margin of 17 or 19 percentage points (depending on whether def 2 or def 1 is used), men are more likely to be sports fans than are women, as shown in Table 2.2.[20] Those in the middle age groups—25-44 and 45-64—are more likely than the youngest and oldest segments to be fans. Minorities (but not persons marking "Other/mixed" as the racial/ethnic category)[21] are more likely than whites to be sports fans. Regional differences are quite muted.

Although not surprising, the sizable gender difference in the incidence of sports fans begs explanation. According to advertising executive Sean McGrath,

> [T]here's something very tribal about guys, especially young guys, that I think sports feeds off of .... I think there's something inherent in guys that they need to gather and they need to have those moments of connection that operate very differently than [among] women.[22]

Table 2.2: Characteristics of Sports Fans, Big4 Fans, and Non-Fans

	Fans of Any College or Pro Sport (definition 2)	Fans of "Big 4" Sport (definition 1)	Non-fans
ALL	77%	72%	23%
Males	86%	81%	14%
Females	69%	62%	31%
Age 18-24	74%	68%	26%
Age 25-44	81%	77%	19%
Age 45-64	78%	72%	22%
Age 65+	71%	63%	29%
White/Caucasian	76%	70%	24%
Black/African-American	79%	77%	21%
Hispanic/Latino*	86%	80%	14%
Asian-American *	81%	76%	19%
Other/mixed*	74%	69%	26%
Northeast	77%	72%	23%
South	76%	68%	24%
Midwest	79%	73%	21%
West	79%	75%	21%

The small numbers of survey respondents in these categories—84 Hispanics/Latinos, 58 Asian-Americans, and 42 Other/mixed—make the percentage estimates in these rows less reliable.

Most fans watch/follow multiple sports.

Most sports fans report following multiple sports; the average number of sports followed is between three and four (3.7 to be exact). As shown in Figure 2.1, fully 83% of fans watch and follow more than one sport. Almost half are fans of four or more sports. Approximately 1 in every 11 fans (9%) watch and follow eight or more different sports. Only about one in six fans specialize by limiting their spectating to one sport.

This multiplicity of fan interests can be explained partly by the great variety of appealing sports competitions available to U.S. consumers and the effectiveness of sports marketing. It is also likely attributable to the high level of leisure time in the

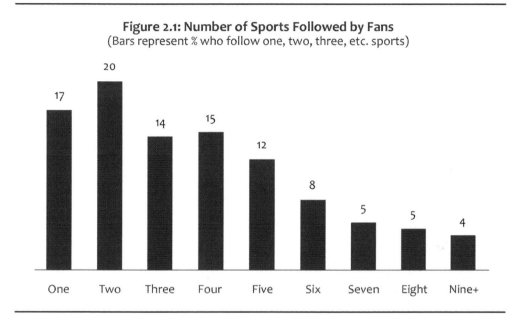

Figure 2.1: Number of Sports Followed by Fans
(Bars represent % who follow one, two, three, etc. sports)

U.S. and, perhaps to a lesser degree, to our relatively high level of disposable income.

Sports fans' favorite sport

One measure of the popularity of different sports is, as used above, the number of people who watch/follow each one. We can also assess spectator popularity by asking survey respondents which of the sports they follow is their *favorite*. By this measure, professional football's dominance is even more dramatic, winning out over baseball (the next most favorite) by a ratio of almost 4 to 1, as shown in Table 2.3.[23]

This ranking is consistent with a series of Harris and Gallup surveys indicating that NFL football has been America's favorite sport at least since the mid-1980s. Other observers trace football's fan dominance to the 1960s.[24]

As impressive as these figures are, the top two dozen elite college football teams are even more popular based on average home field attendance. During the 2015 season, attendance at those teams' games was higher—in some cases far higher—for those 24 college football teams than for every NFL team except the Dallas Cowboys. Even the Cowboys' average game attendance was exceeded by the eight top drawing college teams.[25] To be sure, this is a very different metric than the number of fans in the U.S. who watch and follow those teams and, while intriguing, is heavily dependent on stadium capacity.

Why is NFL football so popular?

To observers of American sports, it should come as no surprise that professional football is our number one spectator sport, dominating in viewer ratings and revenues as well as the sheer percentage of fans who follow it or rate it their favorite. A variety of reasons have been put forth to explain football's popularity. Often heard is football's physically rugged, literally hard-hitting nature. Although many fans might not like to admit it, this "lions in the coliseum" aspect of the game has an appeal which none of the other major sports can match.[26]

Table 2.3: Fans' Favorite Sport to Watch/Follow
Selected from all sports watched/followed
(Base: fans of any college or professional sport)

#	Sport	%
1	NFL football	48%
2	MLB baseball	13%
3	NBA basketball	9%
3	NCAA football	8%
5	NHL hockey	5%
5	Auto racing	5%
7	NCAA basketball	4%
8	Professional soccer	2%
8	Professional tennis	2%
8	Professional golf	2%
	Other/Not sure	2%

A second reason given for professional football's fan dominance is the ease of watching it on television. Not only are more and more games available to watch (mostly without charge), but football's action is ideally suited for the TV screen because, compared to other sports, many things happen at once and must be apprehended visually. In baseball, by contrast, one thing happens at a time, so the action can be communicated orally.[27] It has also become common, if not fashionable, to watch football games together with family and friends—and not only at Super Bowl parties.

Some maintain that football's popularity derives in part from being easy to bet on games, with an abundance of information available about the match-ups and point spreads. The recent explosion of fantasy leagues (not all of which involve gambling) gives fans the opportunity to assemble their own "dream teams"—which adds to the excitement. One-quarter of big4 fans report sometimes betting on sports, and 23% report having participated in a sports fantasy league or contest requiring an entry fee, where they can win money or prizes.

League parity is a logical but rarely heard explanation for football's top-ranked status. Compared to other sports, it is more difficult for NFL owners to assemble a powerhouse lineup, giving many teams about the same chance of rising to the top. This creates a more balanced league and makes it easier for teams to attract fans.[27]

Another reason cited is the skillfully managed and lavishly promoted $9 billion business of NFL football—at least compared to Major League Baseball, its closest competitor. Nevertheless, the game's stellar image (and its attraction) might be starting to show signs of deterioration in part due to the League's nonchalant—some would say negligent—handling of concussions and brain injuries suffered by players.[28] For whatever reason—some attribute it to the surfeit of games being telecast—at the time of this writing (early 2017) NFL TV ratings are down compared to previous years.

We later enumerate and analyze in great depth the reasons given by Sports Fan Survey respondents for the popularity of NFL football.

Summary

1. Sports fandom represents more than mere entertainment. It can be a source of societal integration, but it also has less praiseworthy impacts. Highbrow culture has, at times, denigrated sports fans through condescending stereotypes.

2. More than three-quarters of U.S. adults watch and follow some professional or college sport. About seven of every ten adults are active fans of at least one of the four major professional team sports at the highest level.

3. NFL football has by far the most fans of any sport. Major League Baseball ranks second, followed by NBA basketball, college football, college basketball, NHL hockey, and auto racing.

4. Men are 17 percentage points more likely than women to be fans of some sport at the professional or college level. They are 19 points more likely to be fans of one or more of the major professional team sports.

5. Across the age groups, persons 65 and older are least likely to be sports fans. The youngest segment (18-24) is next least likely to be fans.

6. Racial/ethnic minorities are slightly more likely than whites to be sports fans.

7. The average number of sports that fans watch and follow is between 3 and 4.

8. When asked to name their favorite sport, fans chose NFL football far more than Major League Baseball, NBA basketball, NCAA football, and other sports.

9. One-quarter of big4 fans have bet on sports contests and almost as many have participated in fantasy sports competitions for money.

10. Multiple reasons have been advanced to explain the NFL's popularity including its physicality, easy accessibility to watch on television and as social events, the lure

of betting on games, parity across teams, and the league's extensive marketing efforts. The reasons presented for professional football's dominance are far from exhaustive. I will later present what fans in the Sports Fan Survey themselves say when asked why they like watching professional football (or, if NFL football is not their favorite, whatever other sport it happens to be).

But first we take a look at who watches and follows different sports.

Chapter 3:

Who Follows Which Sports? How Do They Differ?

I always turn to the sports pages first, which records people's
accomplishments. The front page has nothing but man's failures.
– Earl Warren, former U.S. Supreme Court Chief Justice

The previous chapter documented that different sports have vastly different numbers of followers and ranked their overall popularity. But do different sports also attract fans with different demographics? Do women follow professional football as much as men? In appealing to younger fans, does baseball, America's leisurely "national pastime," face hard times ahead competing with faster moving games more in keeping with the pace of contemporary life? Does the NBA attract more African-American fans than other followers? Do fans in different parts of the country have different spectator interests? Are fans of teams in some sports more passionate than others?

When stitched together, the patterns in the data provide profiles of each sport's pool of fans. In some instances, the data support conventional wisdom, but with greater precision than previously available. In other cases, the Sports Fan Survey produces findings that might surprise.

This chapter walks us through the similarities and contrasts of the fans who watch and follow the most popular sports, focusing on gender, age, race/ethnicity, region of residence, and for fans of the big4 sports, education level and strength of identification with their favorite team as well.

Each sport has more male fans than female fans. The NFL is the favorite of both.

Regardless of sport, men are more likely than women to be fans. This is consistent across all ten sports with enough fans for reliable estimates (Figure 3.1). The largest contrasts in terms of the ratio of male fans to female fans are for golf and college basketball, with several sports not far behind. The gender contrasts for tennis and the NFL are the smallest, although still substantial at about 3 men for every 2 women. As it is for men, NFL football is the most popular sport among women fans, as fully half watch it.

Perhaps more unexpected, when big4 sports fans were asked to name their *favorite* spectator sport (not shown in the table), women named NFL football nearly as often as men did—50% to 53.[29]

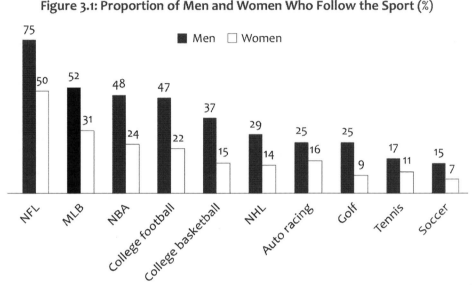

Figure 3.1: Proportion of Men and Women Who Follow the Sport (%)

Most sports appeal more to middle-age fans, but not golf or soccer.

Nearly all sports draw fans disproportionately from the age segments in between the youngest and oldest groups, mostly peaking in the 25-44 age segment (Figure 3.2). The differences are generally small but the pattern is consistent, with golf being the only exception: For golf, the proportion of fans increases regularly with increasing age. NBA fans[30] and soccer fans don't fit this pattern perfectly. For both, the youngest segment (18-24) exceeds the 45-64 year old segment in percentage of fans.

Why are 18-24 year-olds and persons 65 and older generally less likely to be fans? To speculate, it might be that serious "followership" takes some time to develop—that those in the youngest age category are in an impressionable, experimental stage of life when habits and identities are in flux. For some young adults, an absence of interest in a particular sport might result from not having had time to develop an abiding allegiance to a team. Or, their lower interest could be distinctive for that specific cohort of young adults, having grown up in a time of smartphones and video game distractions.

But neither line of thinking explains the lower interest among those of retirement age. In fact, if true, those explanations would lead older people to express *higher*

Figure 3.2: Proportion of Adults That Follow Sport by Age Group (%)

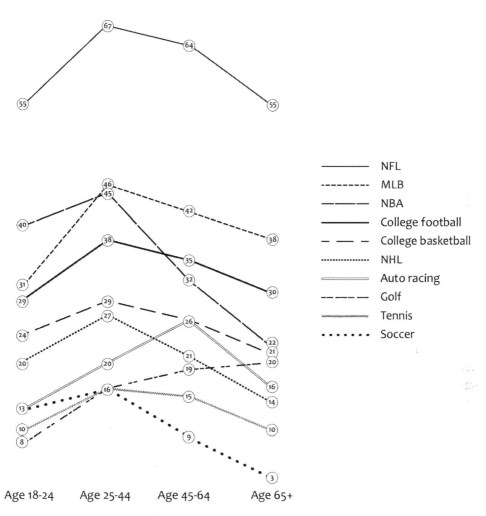

————	NFL		
- - - - - -	MLB		
— — —	NBA		
————	College football		
– — –	College basketball		
··············	NHL		
══════	Auto racing		
- — -- —	Golf		
~~	Tennis		
• • • • • •	Soccer		

Age 18-24   Age 25-44   Age 45-64   Age 65+

interest in spectator sports. Furthermore, most in the oldest segment should also have extra leisure time for following sports. It remains puzzling why persons in this advanced age group (even when limited to sports fans – not broken out separately) should manifest less interest in following most sports. Greater infirmities and lower incomes might initially spring to mind as possible reasons, but neither are compelling explanations.

Baseball fans are older than other fans and the age disparity may be increasing.

The numbers by age group in Figure 3.2 suggest that the youngest segment is less likely to watch/follow baseball than their older counterparts. Another finding from the survey supports the thesis that other sports—football and basketball in particular—might be more popular than baseball among younger adults. When fans were asked to indicate *their favorite sport* among those they watch and follow, more fans in the 65+ age group picked baseball (23%) than did those in the three younger age categories (11-14%).

These indicators from the Sports Fan Survey hardly support definitive forecasts, but neither are they good news for baseball's future. Consistent with these findings and more worrisome for "America's Pastime," other, more extensive data support the conclusion that Major League Baseball has the oldest fans of the four major U.S. professional sports.[31] Susan Jacoby documents how baseball's median viewing age has grown steadily older in recent years, moving from 50½ in 2009 to 54½ in 2013.[32]

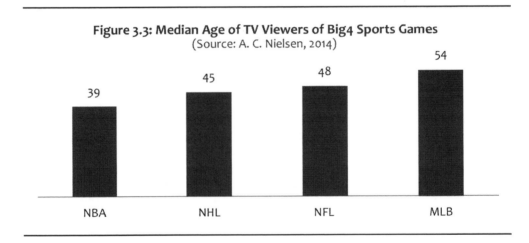

Figure 3.3: Median Age of TV Viewers of Big4 Sports Games
(Source: A. C. Nielsen, 2014)

NBA	NHL	NFL	MLB
39	45	48	54

Jacoby concludes by mentioning how baseball, along with other sports, has benefited from "an explosion in sports rights fees"—$1.5 billion per year in the current TV deal for baseball, extending through 2021—which could be endangered if the average age of viewers continues to rise.[33] Nielsen television ratings (Figure 3.3) provide further evidence of the older average age of baseball fans.

Other data are no less cloudy for baseball's future. Since the 2007-2008 season, average game attendance has leveled off, dropping below 31,000, while team payrolls have continued to rocket upward.[34] Nevertheless, baseball has survived

---

Figure 3.4: Proportions of Whites and African-Americans Who Follow Sport (%)

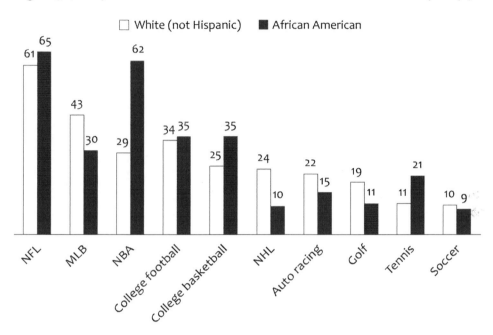

other challenges, such as the use of performance enhancing drugs and the strike shortened 1994 season. Future developments will determine if the trends continue and are sustainable.

African-Americans like baseball, hockey, and golf less; basketball and tennis more.

Ethnic differences in sports spectating abound, as indicated in Figure 3.4, which displays major contrasts in fanship between African-Americans and non-Hispanic whites[35] in at least half of the sports. The racial disparity in the proportions of baseball fans (and players) has received special attention in recent years.

The popularity of baseball as a spectator sport for African-Americans has diminished in line with the declining proportion of black players over the last three decades. Jackie Powell of SBNation cites a study reporting the number of African-Americans on major league rosters as having slid from 18% in 1986 to 8% today.[36] (The African-American share of the 2016 U.S. 18+ age population is 14%.)

Commenting on Chris Rock's bittersweet 2015 comedy routine, where he refers to

African-American baseball fans as an "endangered species,"[37] and in a second SBNation piece bemoaning the situation for black fans, Powell asserts that the African American experience and baseball "do not socialize."[38] He refers to baseball's being "a sport for the rich"[39] and its slow pace as two obstacles hindering greater involvement among young African-Americans. Because of the diminished number of ethnic role models to follow, fewer young blacks develop an interest in the game—a process that, if continued over time, can become a self-reinforcing downward spiral.

African-Americans are also far less likely to follow hockey—a game dominated by Canadians and Europeans at the professional level[40], with few black players. It is only recently that hockey has made inroads in the Southern states, where many blacks live. The relatively steep cost of hockey gear and inaccessibility of ice rinks are further barriers. Only one of the 198 black sports fans participating in the Sports Fan Survey selected hockey as their favorite sport.

Ethnic pride can play a major role in connecting fans to teams, as related in two of the in-depth interviews I conducted. John is a 48 year-old Hispanic in California. He told how his allegiance to the Los Angeles Dodgers was cemented when he got caught up in "Fernando-mania" as Fernando Valenzuela, a relatively obscure left-handed pitcher from Mexico, burst on the scene during the early 1980s. Michelle, originally from Jamaica, works as a home health aide in New York City. She became (and remains) a devoted New York Knicks fan because of Patrick Ewing, also from Jamaica, who played for the Knicks during the late 1980s and 1990s.

When it comes to basketball, a sport in which three-quarters of the players are black[41], African-Americans are *more likely* than whites to follow the game—both the NBA and college versions. They are less likely to follow golf and auto racing, although multiracial Tiger Woods might have increased the number of black golf fans during the peak years of his success. Apart from the appeal of Woods, the dearth of role models and the relative unfamiliarity and expense of golf for many blacks are also barriers to increasing its popularity among African-Americans.

In tennis, a sport not particularly known for attracting African-Americans, at least not until recently, they are ten percentage points more likely than whites to be fans. This is most probably due to the enormous success and popularity of the Williams sisters, Venus and Serena.

Figure 3.5: Proportion of Adults in Each Region Who Follow Each Sport Group (%)

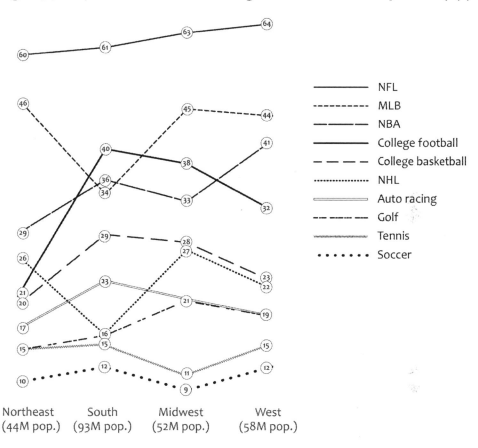

| | Northeast (44M pop.) | South (93M pop.) | Midwest (52M pop.) | West (58M pop.) |

Baseball is less popular in the South than elsewhere.

Baseball is followed less often by Southerners than by residents of other regions (Figure 3.5), primarily because of the scarcity of fans in the East South Central portion of the South (Kentucky, Tennessee, Mississippi, and Alabama). This could be due to the South having fewer Major League Baseball teams relative to its size, and, perhaps more importantly, a shorter tradition of MLB than elsewhere. (The South had no major league team until 1966, when the Braves moved to Atlanta from Milwaukee.)

Nevertheless, because the South has a larger population than the other three Census

Figure 3.6: U.S. Census Regions and Divisions and Regional Adult Population

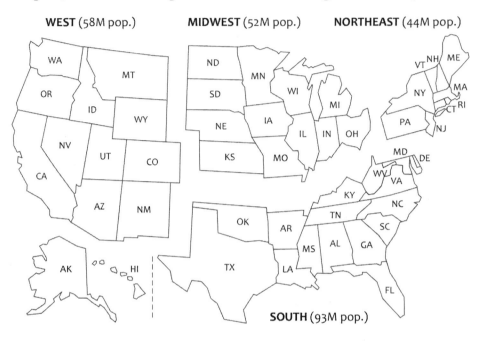

regions (93 million adults) there are more baseball fans there than elsewhere: Nearly one-third of all baseball fans reside in the South, compared to one-quarter in the West, about the same proportion in the Midwest, and approximately one-fifth in the Northeast.

Adults/fans in the West are more likely than in other regions to follow the NBA.

More than 40% of adults living in the West watch and follow NBA basketball. Those in the West are the most likely to be NBA fans, and persons residing in the Northeast are the least likely to be. The NBA's popularity in the West could be partly due to the recent emergence of the Golden State Warriors as a successful and exciting franchise. As will be seen later, the Warriors were named as basketball fans' favorite team a disproportionate number of times, as were even more the Los Angeles Lakers, despite the latter's lack of recent success.

The relatively low popularity of the NBA in the Northeast might reflect the hard times experienced of late by historically storied teams like the New York Knicks, the

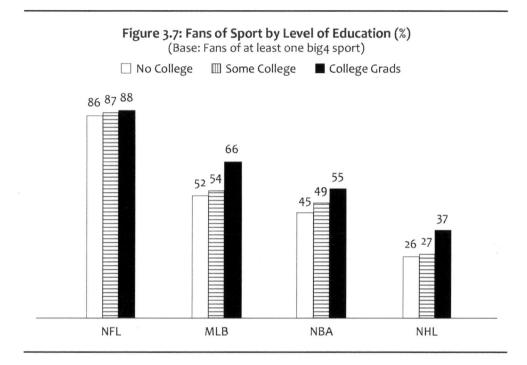

Figure 3.7: Fans of Sport by Level of Education (%)
(Base: Fans of at least one big4 sport)

☐ No College   ▦ Some College   ■ College Grads

Philadelphia 76ers, and to a lesser degree, the Boston Celtics.

Despite that the largest percentage who watch and follow professional basketball live in the West, because of its larger population the South has more NBA fans (38% of all) than the West (27%), the Midwest (20%), and the Northeast (15%). This mirrors the situation in baseball.

Hockey is most popular in the Midwest and Northeast.

The flip side of pro basketball's low popularity in the Northeast is hockey's strong showing in that region of the country. More than one-quarter of all adults in the Northeast are hockey fans. Historically, most NHL teams were situated there (or even further North, in Canada). Hockey's strong showing in the Northeast is equaled if not exceeded slightly among Midwesterners. Because of hockey's unequal regional population distribution, the fan base of the NHL is quite evenly divided across the four regions.

College football is least popular in the Northeast.

College football has the most followers in the South and Midwest—and is least popular by far in the Northeast, which has traditionally favored private and smaller schools less likely to have extensive or nationally successful football programs. And, with few exceptions (Penn State being the most notable), public universities in the Northeast are small compared to those in other regions.

Other regional contrasts

College basketball is less popular in the Northeast and West than in the South and Midwest. Auto racing is most popular in the South and Midwest. Golf as a spectator sport is less popular in the Northeast and South compared to the Midwest and West. Tennis is least popular in the Midwest.

College graduates are most likely to be fans of a professional sports team (except possibly an NFL team)

Consistent with NFL football's strong popularity among all segments, it is uniformly popular regardless of education level. The same cannot be said of baseball, which exhibits higher popularity among sports fans who are college graduates, as does hockey and basketball (Figure 3.7).[42]

The higher popularity among college graduates for at least three of the four sports is somewhat of a mystery, although findings from other studies are consistent.[43] One might speculate that it results from college graduates having higher incomes and possibly more free time, enabling those fans to be heavier consumers of baseball, hockey, and/or basketball, whereas football's popularity is so high and widespread that "ceiling effects" block any correlation with other factors.[44]

Are baseball fans less passionate than other fans?

Before closing this chapter, one additional fan characteristic warrants attention— strength of identification with one's favorite team. In addition to watching sporting events to enjoy suspenseful outcomes or esthetic performances by teams they are unattached to, viewers more often watch because of their emotional commitment to a favorite team—part of a basic human tendency to identify with a larger group.[45] Sometimes extreme emotional attachment gets expressed as fanaticism.[46]

After fans were asked in the survey to name their favorite team in each sport they follow, they were asked which one of the teams in the sports they follow is their favorite *overall*. We end with a look at whether fans whose overall favorite team plays baseball (or football, basketball, or hockey) are stronger identifiers—are more psychologically invested—in their team than fans of teams in the other sports.[47]

In other words, do the data support the possibility that fans of teams in some professional sports are more passionate or less passionate than other fans? Although psychological identification and passion are not equivalent, they overlap enough to be used here synonymously.

To measure identification with team, we draw upon the Sport Spectator Identification Scale (SSIS),[48] developed and applied by psychologists in dozens

It is no coincidence that the Latin origin of the term "fan" means "fanatic", or ardent devotee. This interpretation has been disputed by historian Peter Morris, who suggests it might be from the hand-held fans that bleacherites waved to cool themselves or to the flapping of their tongues, which can sound like the whirring of fans.[47]

of research studies. The seven statements that make up the SSIS capture different dimensions of fan identification with team, such as how important it is that the team wins, how strongly you see yourself as a fan of the team, how closely you follow the team, etc. The cumulative SSIS score is a validated measure of the extent to which fans associate themselves with their favorite team in terms of interests, values, and actions.

An initial comparison of SSIS scores by fans with differing favorite professional team sports suggests that baseball fans (fans whose overall favorite team plays baseball) identify slightly less with their favorite team—are a little less passionate about them— than fans of teams in the other three sports. At first glance, this observed contrast seems to accord with popular perceptions. While fans at the ballpark can certainly get worked up and cheer wildly at critical moments, most observers familiar with this quartet would probably feel that fans of hockey, football, and basketball are typically a rowdier, if not more frenzied lot than baseball fans.

This provocative finding led me to dig deeper to try to understand the reason for this difference. As it turns out, (1) the SSIS scores show that men *generally* identify more strongly than women with their favorite team; (2) the same is true to an even greater degree, among fans under 60 compared to the oldest segment;[49] and (3) fans whose favorite team is a baseball team include proportionately more women and more fans 60 and older than those whose favorite is a football, basketball, or hockey team.

In short, Major League Baseball's distinctive demographic profile—its relatively higher proportion of women and older fans—accounts for why its fans identify a little less strongly than other fans.[50] The contrast Is probably not a result of weaker responses elicited by the game of baseball per se.

Summary

This chapter has uncovered many patterns and contrasts among the fans of different sports. We close with a summary of the main take-aways:

1. NFL football commands a large proportion of fans. It appeals to, and is the favorite sport of, a broad swatch of demographic segments.

2. Female sports fans are less likely than male fans to watch and follow every sport asked about.

3. Women are nearly as likely as men to name NFL football as their favorite professional team sport.

4. Baseball is least popular among the youngest segment of adults, and it is far less popular among this group than football and basketball. TV viewing data suggest that the average age of baseball fans is increasing.

5. NBA basketball is more popular among younger adults and younger sports fans than among adults and fans 45+.

6. Unlike for other sports, the percentage who watch and follow golf increases steadily with age and is highest among the oldest segment.

7. African-Americans are much more likely than whites to be basketball and tennis fans, are less likely to be baseball fans, and are especially less likely to be hockey fans.

8. Baseball is least popular percentage-wise in the South. NBA basketball is most popular in the West region. NHL hockey is most popular in the Midwest and Northeast.

9. College football has the most followers percentage-wise in the South and Midwest; it is least popular by far in the Northeast. College basketball enjoys higher popularity in the South and Midwest than the West and Northeast. Auto racing is also most popular in the South and Midwest.

10. College graduates (those having a Bachelor's degree or the equivalent) are more likely than non-graduates to be professional baseball, basketball, and hockey fans.

11. Fans whose favorite professional team sport is baseball tend to identify slightly less with their favorite baseball team than fans who favorite is football, basketball, or hockey. Deeper analysis finds that this is very likely due to the different gender and age profiles of baseball's fans rather than to something intrinsic to baseball.

12. With the possible exception of hockey fans, we found that women generally identify less strongly with their favorite team than males do, and that persons in their 60s and older also tend to identify with their favorite less strongly than younger fans.

Chapter 4:

Theories of Fan Attachments

*I'm convinced that we care because the games we love offer
immeasurable opportunity to be included in something
more than just a workforce or a family unit.*
– Chip Scarinzi *in Diehards: Why Fans Care So Much About Sports*

The last two chapters focused on comparing sports fans and non-fans as well as estimating their numbers, and analyzing how the various fan segments, defined by which sports they watch and follow, differ from one another. Our attention moving forward centers on trying to account for why people become sports fans, prefer one of the big4 sports the most, and why they favor one team over its competitors.

We begin by introducing three theories that might help explain sports interests and team attachments. These theories are best viewed as overlapping accounts which share elements in common rather than as wholly discrete, competing models. The chapter concludes with a list of plausible—and more directly testable—factors offered to describe why we like particular sports and teams.

1. Sports fandom as religious attachment

Much has been written about the religious quality of sports fans' attraction to their team. As one author puts it, "Sports and religion both serve to bring like-minded people together in celebration of oneness and community."[51] Commenting on the emotional fervor expressed while watching football—the same could be said for watching other sports—writer and philosopher Michael Novak asserts that sports fandom derives from a deep impulse that is radically religious.[52]

In *The Joy of Sports* he makes the case that sports are more like religion than mere entertainment by describing how animated fans become watching games on television, referring to football as a prime example, and how it has a unique way of involving the spirit.[53] He contends that "Sports owe more to the ritual grammar of religion than to the laws and forms of entertainment. More become involved in the rituals of sport to a depth of seriousness never elicited by entertainment."[54]

Extending the metaphor, Novak views the time set aside for watching sports as sacred time, different and apart from everyday normal routines. "Sacred time is full of exhilaration, excitement, and peace, as though it were more real and more joyous than the activities of everyday life—as though it were *really living* to be in sacred time (wrapped up in a close game)."[55]

Unlike Novak, who is Catholic and writes from a Catholic perspective, Michael Mandelbaum, a Jewish academic who writes mostly about foreign policy, makes remarkably similar points. He observes out how both sports and religion "address the needs of the spirit and the psyche rather than those of the flesh ... [and how] both stand outside the working world." He comments how watching team sports provides three things that before the modern age only religion offered: "a welcome diversion from the routines of daily life; a model of coherence and clarity; and heroic examples to admire and emulate."[56]

Evolutionary psychologist Nigel Barber further expands on the commonalities by noting how the rituals of sport can resemble those of religion:

> Fans wear the team colors and carry its flags, icons, and mascots. Then there is repetitive chanting of team encouragement, hand-clapping, booing the other team, doing the wave, and so forth. The singing of an anthem at a sporting event likely has similar psychological effects as the singing of a hymn in church.[57]

Psychologist Daniel Wann and his collaborators describe the similarity of vocabulary used in religion and sport: faith, devotion, worship, ritual, dedication, sacrifice, commitment, spirit, prayer, suffering, festival, and celebration. They make the case that sports fandom, like religion, can provide the social cohesion which "... binds people together through ritual and belief by offering common values and goals toward which they may strive." They also note the correspondence between diminishing church attendance and expanding attendance at sporting events in recent years, suggesting that the two institutions might perform complementary, if not interchangeable, functions in society.[58]

Other researchers see sports as a "humanistic religion" in which spectators worship other human beings, their achievements, and the groups [teams] to which they belong,[59] and compare sports stadiums and arenas to cathedrals where followers gather to worship their heroes and pray for their success.[60]

Allegiance to a favorite team can be as strong as adherence to one's faith. As Maureen, a retired social worker in Massachusetts, replied when I asked if she could imagine herself ever abandoning the Red Sox to root for a different baseball team: "It's kind of like the Catholic church for me. I'm not entirely happy with the church right now, just as I'm occasionally angry at the team's owners. But I could never leave."

Wann et al forecast that the "religious importance" of sports spectating will intensify at both the individual and societal levels as societies grow increasingly more secular and theological beliefs become less salient.[61]

While this line of argument is thought provoking, the authors' prediction strikes me as a bit of a stretch. As the old saw goes: Correlation does not necessarily imply causation. Just because declining traditional religiosity and the increasing significance of sports have been related in time does not mean that intensified sports spectating is serving as a substitute for religion's decline. Nevertheless, the parallels remain intriguing, and the idea that fandom might be a substitute for declining traditional social ties provided by religion (and possibly other institutions, such as family) deserves considered attention.

2. Quest for community through non-religious affiliation

Related to the diminished role played by traditional religion in providing community is the innate human search for belongingness through attachment to a group of like-minded members—what might be succinctly referred to as a form of modern day tribalism. It is often rightly said that it is natural for humans to join groups of all kinds—not just religious ones. Our sharing of beliefs and ideas is what helps us be group animals.[62] Whether religious or secular, sharing positive emotional experiences in the presence of others enhances the experience.

Although attachment to a religious community might also be viewed as a form of tribalism, traditional religion relies upon a shared set of deeper theological or supernatural beliefs, or morally sanctioned practices in a way that non-religious community does not require. The latter can be purely secular and social in purpose.

Many have lamented the decline of traditional family life, the fraying of institutional loyalties, the rapid pace of technological change, the rise of the global economy, and other sources of community decline (besides the loosening of attachments to church).[63] Attaching oneself to a sports team as a dedicated fan can be a way of making friends and achieving community for those who are lonely or isolated—in some cases although not necessarily—as a result of macro societal changes.

Diehards author Skip Scarinzi is convinced that the desire for community and camaraderie is the main reason people become sports fans:

> In the same way that excitement may spike slightly when you come across someone at a party who might have seen and enjoyed the same movie you saw, sports fandom brings people together in celebration of a common interest … [64]

The profusion of Facebook pages and blogs started by fans attests to the desire of loyalists to share their interest and enthusiasm for their favorite team. Indeed, more than one-third of the fans in my recent Sports Fan Survey had participated in an online discussion about their favorite team in the past 12 months, or had posted comments about them on social media or a website.

In their introduction to *Sports Mania*, Hugenberg, Haridakis, and Earnheardt contend "[Sports fans] are doing more than just sharing and discussing sports. They are building community and social capital. Sports bring people together."[65] A compelling example of the social integration function of sports is Joseph Epstein's story, cited earlier, about how an interest in sports was the sole source of the mutual fellowship which he (a highly sophisticated writer from New York City) experienced working in the South among other men with whom he shared little else in common.

Reflecting on the experience watching his first Notre Dame football game in South Bend, writer and Fighting Irish fan Joe Queenan expresses it in his inimical style:

> Supporting a particular team and vilifying its opponents necessitated an inexplicable bonding process whereby an army of complete strangers alchemically metamorphosed into one's sworn kinsmen.[66]

The vilification Queenan mentions represents the darker side of group affiliation—drawing sharp distinctions between your group and competitors—which not infrequently occurs and can sometimes morph into fierce antipathy or violence in extreme cases. Much research on sports fans has focused on this form of less savory behavior, most notably as manifested in international soccer hooliganism but also the extreme actions of U.S. sports fans, particularly when occasioned by contests between long-time bitter rivals.

Tribalism can shape how fans of competing teams can view the same event in diametrically opposite ways. In an incident during game 3 of the 2nd round 2017 NHL playoff series between the Washington Capitals and the Pittsburgh Penguins, Penguins' star center Sidney Crosby suffered a concussion from a blow to the head by the Washington Capitals' Matt Niskanen. The Washington Post's Dan Steinberg reports how intelligent, respectable Pittsburgh partisans (including long-time professional observers of the game) saw the crosscheck to Crosby's head as an intentional, dirty blow, while their Capitals' counterparts viewed it as unfortunate but accidental.

Steinberg quotes Howard Lavine, a professor at the University of Minnesota specializing in political psychology, to help explain these contrasting interpretations:

> We sincerely believe that we saw what we think we saw... The idea of being

motivated to be a member of a group is partly a function of wanting that group to be seen as different and better. That means you want your team to win, yes, but it also suggests you want your team infused with nobility and honor.[67]

According to Lavine, this tendency is built into us through evolution.

3. Identification with team

A third approach to understanding spectator attachment to sports teams can be found in the processes of psychological identification.[68] This view focuses more on purely psychological processes than the interpersonal quest for community or spirituality, although they share common elements. While fans vary a lot in their degree of identification—some view attributes of the team they like as part of their self concept more than others do (as shown, for example, by the variation in SSIS scores in the previous chapter)—it is almost by definition impossible to maintain interest in a team with which a person shares few qualities or no important singular quality. For fans who identify strongly with a team, the role of team follower is a central component of their identity.[69]

Identifying with a sport or a team can be an important source of pride and self-worth, especially when it is popular or looked upon favorably by one's peers. It can also powerfully enhance one's sense of belonging. As researchers have found, team identification is quite stable, with fans reporting consistent levels over time. Strongly identified fans often view their team (and its performance) as a reflection of themselves. The team becomes an extension of the individual. The team's successes become the fan's successes and the team's failures become the fan's failures.[70]

Degree of identification has been shown to influence various aspects of fan behavior and psychological health including self-esteem. "Basking in reflected glory" (or BIRGing, as it is referred to in the research literature) is one of the ways fans build their self-esteem. Identifying with a team is something we do to feel better about ourselves.[71]

According to Eric Simons, author of *The Secret Life of Sports Fans*, what most defines a sports fan is the "ability to form a meaningful, quasi-relationship" with a team—a deep psychological connection with it. He points to research that shows "the depth of the relationship makes it go and provides the meaning and pride." Simons draws upon recent scientific research to describe how neuron mirroring in the brain helps explain and perpetuate team identification.[72]

His main point: A sports fan's relationship with a team, although vicarious and one-sided, can fulfill human needs just like an inter-personal relationship. While noting how much sports psychology has focused on aggression and violence, he offers a novel counter-idea—by observing sports fans, we can learn as much about how and why humans form groups, love each other, and commit altruistic acts as about conflict and division. Simons quotes UC-Berkeley psychologist Rudy Mendoza-Denton, who says it tells us something about our fundamental need to belong.[73] In this respect, social identity theory overlaps quest for community.

A stunning illustration of identification with team—by an entire community, not just an individual—is given by travel writer Paul Theroux, about his visit to Tuscaloosa, Alabama, home of the University of Alabama and their famed football team the Crimson Tide: "Football is the town's identity, and the game makes its citizens happy—resolves their conflicts, unifies them, helps them forget their pain, gives them membership in a cult of winners. 'Football is religion here,' some Tuscaloosans also say."[74]

He goes on to acknowledge how most cities are proud of their sports teams but is struck by the heightened intensity in Tuscaloosa from the "processions of cars flying battle flags, the whooping and the costumes," the filled stadium, and the tattoos and chants, which he analogizes to a defiant people asserting their tribal identity.[75] *

Theroux accounts for this group behavior by referencing the aforementioned social identity theory, in which people attach themselves to groups as a source of pride and self-esteem. Groups provide a sense of social identity and belonging. For some, it can matter so much that it provides a purpose in life. For avid fans, this attachment means you're more than a passive member of the group; you're an active booster, helping make the team bigger and stronger. According to social identity theorists, we increase our self-image by enhancing the status of the groups we belong to.[76]

• In the early, testing phase of my research, I coincidentally came upon a Crimson Tide fan in his early 30s whose attachment reveals a unique twist on social identity theory. Now living in San Francisco, this young man grew up "as a closeted kid" [his words] in a white middle-class family in what he described as a "horrible, conservative town" in Alabama, which he yearned to escape from. His family consisted mostly of life-long Crimson Tide football fans, from whom he inherited an initial loyalty to the team—an allegiance cemented by being one of the few things about his state which, in his view, commands national admiration and respect.

But that doesn't fully explain his intense allegiance. From his early teens, when he began to realize there exists a broader, more appealing world outside of his parochial town, he looked to the university in Tuscaloosa as his best way out. Crimson Tide football became a constant reminder that "I'm going to get out of there. I'm not going to be stuck in this town." He did end up graduating from the University of Alabama. Now, more than a decade later, he looks back on the school and everything associated with it—most notably, the football team—with the fondest memories and deepest team attachment, as indeed in a symbolic and real way it became his ticket to leave.

Theroux's observations illustrate how elements of the three models of sports fandom can complement each other—the analogy with religious attachment, the secular desire for community, and the psychological benefits conveyed in the form of enhanced self-esteem.

Eric Simons produced a popular account of how psychological effects of following a team, which can be intense, stem from *physiological* processes. The main theme is summarized in a newspaper story about the research he conducted for *The Secret Life of Sports Fans*:

> A sports team is an expression [and expansion] of a fan's sense of self ...
> It is not an obnoxious affectation when a devotee uses the word "we"; it's a literal confusion in the brain about what is "me" and what is "the team" ... Self-esteem rides on the outcome of the game and the image of the franchise.[77]

Other theories/motivations of sports fans

The three theories just outlined are not the only approaches to understanding what motivates sports fans. The others, some of which are alluded to elsewhere in this volume, are of varying validity, sophistication, and utility—entertainment, thrill seeking, escape, bonding with family, catharsis (of aggressive impulses), acquisition of knowledge, economic motives (sports betting), and appreciation/veneration of values such as teamwork, perseverance, character, and so forth. Thorough description and evaluation of these other ideas are beyond the scope of this book. Readers wishing to explore them further might consult Sloan and Van Camp's article in *Sports Mania*.[78]

Yet another possible driver of fan attachments, suggested by one of my reviewers, is the *search for meaning* in delimited contests, and the related *search for clarity*, when so much in life seems pointless or random. Becoming invested in games with concrete rules, finite ends, and black-and-white results can be comforting when so much is beyond our understanding.

Digression: Why some fans root for perennial losing teams

Identity theory would seem hard pressed to account for why some sports fans maintain their allegiances to teams with long-term losing records. Is this simply a manifestation of masochistic behavior, or is something else going on?

One intriguing answer lies in the idea of "effort justification," as described by Jon L. Wertheim and Sam Sommers in *This is Your Brain On Sports*. It's really quite simple:

Fans continue cheering on losing teams year after year to vindicate their extended misery by anticipating the blissful psychic rewards when the team finally achieves greatness—rewards which will be all the sweeter because it took so long to attain them. When people make sacrifices to pursue a goal, the effort exerted is often validated by elevating the attractiveness of the goal.[79]

The exquisiteness of the future satisfaction that await these fans will, in a sense, rationalize the failure and suffering endured: "[W]hen you root for a perennial loser and it finally wins, the experience is suffused with joy and importance ... And if and when the long-suffering team wins ... all that effort is really justified."[80]

Of course, some fans stick with losing teams for other reasons such as history, tradition, civic pride, and attachments of significant others. Also, many fans take pride in their unwavering loyalty, finding the alternative of flitting from team to team depending on what team is currently winning or otherwise in fashion—the practice of so-called "bandwagon fans"—to be repugnant.

Stressing the positive in fan loyalty, Emily in Arizona, 27, an Oakland Raiders fan (soon to be Las Vegas Raiders), put it this way: "Rooting for a team even when they're bad says a lot about someone's character ... You want to be on the right side when someone tries to call you a fair-weather fan."

According to Ben Berkon, for some fans "The camaraderie of losing actually supersedes the sanctity of winning.[81] He quotes Michael Serby, professor of psychiatry at the Icahn School of Medicine at Mount Sinai Hospital, who says some fans wear their allegiance to a losing team as a badge of honor. The term for this is Basking in Reflected Failure (BIRFing), which occurs when individuals who identify with a team that consistently fails to win maintain their membership status.[82]

Indeed, as presented later, pride in loyalty to one's team is a sentiment often expressed by respondents in the Sports Fan Survey—perhaps not so dissimilar to rooting for the underdog, a motivation voiced by small but distinctive segment of fans. As noted, it can produce a firm bond from sharing that pride and the experiences that give rise to it with other diehards.

Transitioning to the data analysis: possible sources of sports interests and team allegiances

As noted in the introduction, although one's initial attraction to a sport is more likely to precede attachment to a particular team, the opposite is also possible. Youngsters growing up in or near Washington DC, for example, might develop an interest in watching football from prior identification with the media saturated Washington Redskins. Similarly, an interest in baseball might be driven by living in the Boston area, where the Red Sox are broadly worshipped.

While in reality it might be difficult to untangle fans' interest in particular sports from their attachment to a particular team, these are analytically separable and separately researchable. One can propose any number of reasons for developing a spectator interest in baseball, hockey, golf, or other sports. It could stem from a parent's or older sibling's enthusiasm, or, typically later in life, from the attachment of a spouse or significant other. In many instances a fan's interest might derive from having played the game when younger or, less commonly, from having taken up the game as an adult.

A comprehensive list of precursors of spectator interest should also include fascination with the athleticism or aesthetics displayed in a sport, the thrill and excitement of the action and competition, or possibilities of record-setting achievements. Others might be drawn to watching a sport because it affords opportunities for social interaction or bonding with family and friends (as implied in the quest for community concept). Still others are attracted as spectators for the opportunity to escape from the daily rigors and stresses of life. For a smaller number of fans, their interest might be sustained by opportunities to win money or gain bragging rights in fantasy game competition or from plain old-fashioned betting on games.[83]

Lastly, although they might not acknowledge it or even be conscious of it, some fans likely follow a sport because, as implied in social identity theory, they share/ admire certain qualities or values believed embedded in the sport's success, such as athleticism, strength, aggressiveness, speed, courage, endurance, risk-taking, strategic skills, and so forth. These various sources of fan attachment will be directly examined in the data analysis to follow.

For me, an even more intriguing question is the origin and persistence of preferences for particular *teams*. As a framework for examining how team allegiances arise and change over time, many of the reasons just enumerated for explaining interest in particular sports should also serve. Based on previous research,[84] I expect, in particular, that socialization by family and friends, opportunities for pleasurable group experiences, and a desire for belonging or "community," will supplement geographic proximity and go a long way toward helping explain why fans select particular teams as their favorites. Nevertheless, there are other factors that need to be added to this list—factors which only make sense in the context of accounting for favorite *teams*:

- Team success
- Popularity of specific players (hero worship in the case of a few superstars)
- Identifying with or wishing to show support for a particular city or region
- Perceived values or behavior of the team's players, coaches, and owners
- Accessibility of watching/following the team—in person or otherwise
- Idiosyncratic—some would say superficial—features such as the team's name, uniforms, logo, or mascot.

These sources of team attachment will also be examined in the data analysis.

In the next chapter, we turn again to the Sports Fan Survey to find out why fans like their favorite professional team sport. Subsequent chapters then examine what they like about being a fan of their favorite team and how team attachments originate.

Chapter 5:

Why Fans Like Their Favorite Team Sport

[I like] the bone-crushing sounds when they smack into each other.
  – 48 year-old Florida woman explaining why she likes football best

The best stand-up comedy routine about sports is George Carlin's riff on the contrasts between baseball and football, In his sketch, Carlin presents an extended series of contrasts between America's two premier games, suggesting that football is tense, conflictual, and warlike, while baseball is a more relaxed, friendly, and gentler contest:

> *Baseball is a nineteenth-century pastoral game. Football is a twentieth-century technological struggle... In football you wear a helmet. In baseball you wear a cap... Football has hitting, clipping, spearing, piling on, personal fouls, late hitting and unnecessary roughness. Baseball has the sacrifice...* [85]

Reading the text, even the full routine, does not do justice to Carlin's masterful live performance, which can be viewed on YouTube.[86] His intent was to tell us something about ourselves and our values. As such, his poetic comparisons suggest some subtle and some not so subtle distinctions between the games, and by implication, to the types of fans each game appeals to.

Not everyone is as hard on football as Carlin. Michael Novak's spin on football's war-relevant virtues, for instance, is more affirmative, praising football for teaching teamwork, concentration, discipline, and preparedness for the unexpected.[87]

By exploring why fans like their favorite professional team sport, this chapter seeks to characterize the appeal that different sports have for their fans. The objective is to determine if and how baseball and football differ, as Carlin's droll portrayal suggests and, at the same time, adding comparisons about basketball's appeal to NBA fans and hockey's appeal to NHL fans.

Chapter roadmap

So far, we've estimated the numbers of fans of different sports, highlighted their similarities and differences, and introduced theories suggesting reasons why fans might be attracted to certain sports and teams. The focus now shifts to examining sports fans and fan segments from a different perspective—by analyzing and illustrating what they like about their favorite sport. To convey the richness and variety

Table 5.1: Categories Used to Summarize Fans' Responses About Why They Like Their Favorite Sport

Category (% of fans expressing this type of response[89])	Description
Engaging (44%)	Typically enthusiastic responses to watching the sport: exciting, dramatic, suspenseful, competitive, intense, high energy, strategic, action packed, fast paced; high-level athleticism/skill of players noted
Team/Place (20%)	Like the sport because of a specific team (usually one's favorite team) or players on that team; like city, my city/state, accessible (close)
My tradition (11%)	Always liked, liked for a long time, evokes long-ago memories, family tradition, memories watching with family/friends, grew up watching
Just like (10%)	Like, love, fun, great, best, interesting, enjoyable, entertaining; other positive but typically vague, succinct responses not explaining why the sport is liked
Family/Social (8%)	Enjoy watching and following with family/friends, family or friends like sport, like discussing sport
Played (6%)	Played that sport when younger, play that sport now
Physical (5%)	Hard-hitting, tough/rough game, "man's game"
Players (3%)	Like players in sport, know players, have favorite player(s)
Easy to follow (3%)	Easy to understand/follow, know the rules
Values (3%)	Embodies/teaches important values, like values of my team, American
Civil, slower, human scale (2%)	Not (as) violent, human scale (needn't be big/tall/strong), slower paced
Other (8%)	All other intelligible responses not falling into one of other categories
Blank/uncodable (8%)	No answer or unintelligible response

of the comments, I include extensive examples of answers given in respondents' own words to the Sports Fan Survey's open-ended query: *Why do you like to watch/follow [FAVORITE BIG4 SPORT]? What is it that appeals to you?*

Themes detected in fans' answers

The responses ranged in length from one or two words to short paragraphs. Each response was carefully reviewed and "coded," that is, placed into up to three categories (codes) that capture its essential meaning(s).[88] The 13 categories shown below were developed to summarize what fans like about their favorite sport (including an "all other" category for idiosyncratic answers and those not fitting elsewhere).

Note: The percentages shown in Table 5.1 and Figure 5.1 indicate the proportion of respondents whose answer was assigned a code in the respective category—NOT the proportion of all codes assigned. The percentages sum to more than 100% because multiple codes were assigned when necessary to account for multiple themes in some respondents' answers.

Figure 5.1 is a graphic representation of Table 5.1, providing a visual depiction of the incidence of the various themes expressed in respondents' answers.

Breaking down the categories by fans with different favorite sports

For the purpose of this chapter, these overall percentages might be less informative than the breakdown of the various types of responses by fans with different favorite sports. To help understand the appeals of each sport, we show how many NFL, MLB, NBA, and NHL fans like their favorite sport for each reason. Do the appeals of the various sports differ? If they do, in what ways and to what extent? The substantively meaningful contrasts in Table 5.2 are noted in the discussion that follows.

Illustrations of what fans like about their favorite sport

Quoting respondents' verbatim answers illustrates how sports fans think and talk about the sports they follow. They are just as revealing as the statistical data and comparisons across the different sports.

1. My favorite sport is engaging. ("Engaging" - 44% of fans)

The most common reason given about what fans like about their favorite sport— *although notably not by baseball fans*—is being emotionally or cognitively engaged by the game. These answers included words such as "exciting," "suspenseful," "competitive," "intense," "strategic," "fast paced," "high energy," "talented

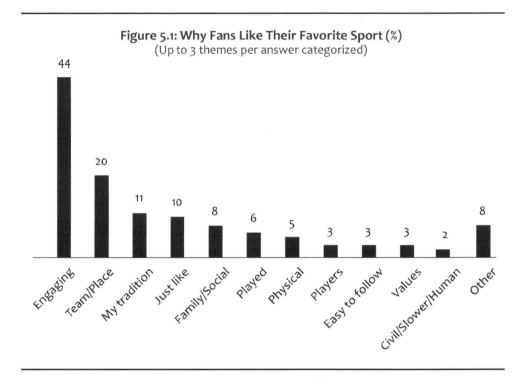

Figure 5.1: Why Fans Like Their Favorite Sport (%)
(Up to 3 themes per answer categorized)

athletes," and similar adjectives in describing what it is about their favorite professional team sport that engages them. To merit this code, respondents had to give some such specific reason why they find their preferred sport engaging, rather than to say merely and vaguely that they "like" it, "it's great," "the best," "interesting," or "enjoyable" (terms that only beg why). It excludes answers like "rough," "tough," and "hard-hitting," which merit its own, separate category (**physical**) described later.

A sport's capacity to engage its audience has several sub-themes, which are described and illustrated in the following paragraphs.

Abundant action or fast pace is especially prominent among hockey fans. Fans liking NHL hockey the most often mention its action or fast pace. Football fans and basketball fans mention it less than hockey fans. Almost no baseball fans cite this as a reason why they like baseball. Here are some examples of this type of response[91]:

> [I like hockey because of the] constant action, [and because it's a]
> fast-paced, high-energy sport that lacks the down-time of baseball.
> – 34 year-old male from Illinois

Table 5.2: What Fans Like About Their Favorite Sport[90]
(% of fans citing each reason*)

	Football (NFL) (809 fans)	Baseball (MLB) (223 fans)	Basketball (NBA) (169 fans)	Hockey (NHL) (86 fans)
Engaging	48	24	43	65
Team/Place	19	27	15	15
My tradition	10	23	8	4
Just like	11	7	12	10
Family/Social	10	7	1	3
Played	4	12	13	3
Physical	7	< 0.5	0	14
Players	2	3	7	3
Easy to follow	2	8	4	3
Values	2	7	5	0
Civil, slower, human scale	< 0.5	8	1	0
Other	8	12	4	7
Blank/uncodable	9	7	11	1

The column percentages sum to more than 100% because the responses could contain more than one reason/theme.

I like the continuous action and excitement [of basketball] …
Also the dunks and alley-oops.
  – New York man, 51

[NFL football is] action packed and nail-biting exciting.
  – 54 year-old South Carolina woman

Other comments refer to the sport's **excitement or intensity** (without necessarily mentioning action or pace). Psychologists who study sports fandom refer to the "eustress" motivation—positive forms of arousal and stimulation viewers seek from watching exciting sports.[92]

It is so very exciting and keeps you on the edge of your seat.
  – 58 year-old New York man who likes NFL football the best

The intensity and the amazing NBA players.
 – Asian-American woman in California, 33

[NFL football] gets the blood pumping and is a riot to watch.
 – 50 year-old Tennessee man

Hay muchas emociones y pasiones. (There is a lot of passion and emotion.)
 – Hispanic male baseball fan, 34, in Ohio

Players' exceptional physical virtuosity was also often noted as a reason why watching one's favorite professional team sport is engaging. **Athletic talent** was mentioned proportionately more often by fans designating basketball or hockey as their favorite.

I love following the Thunder, our local team. Kevin Durant and Russell Westbrook are amazing athletes. [Note: Durant was a member of the Thunder at the time of the survey.]
 – 56 year-old Oklahoma woman

[I like] ... how great an athlete a hockey player is.
 – 75 year-old man in New Mexico

I like the athleticism of the players.
 – 27 year-old African-American male football fan from Michigan

The players ... truly have talent.
 – 22 year-old male hockey fan from Missouri

As Buck O'Neill, a manager in the old baseball Negro Leagues, so perfectly put it:

You can have two 80 year-old men sitting on the couch watching a baseball game, and a guy drops a pop fly. The first words that come out their mouth is, 'I could have caught that' ... If LeBron James misses a dunk, everybody ain't saying 'I could have done that!'[93]

Meaningful games, close games, unpredictable games

This attribute was particularly prominent among NFL football fans. One contributing factor, although hardly the only reason, is fewer games than in the other three sports, so each one has a greater effect on the standings and chances to make the playoffs.

Things can change at the last minute.
 – Female football fan, 46, from Missouri

There are fewer games [than the other sports], which makes each game more important and exciting.
 – 32 year-old male football fan from West Virginia

You never know when your team will win or suck.
  – 40 year-old woman from Tennessee who favors football

There's so much parity nowadays [in the NFL].
  – 52 year-old male in upstate New York

This last response focuses on a less often discussed factor contributing to the unpredictability of NFL game outcomes—the greater parity of teams across the league compared to other sports. It was mentioned in Chapter 2 as one reason for NFL football's huge popularity. Two factors accounting for this are the NFL's salary cap and its revenue sharing model.

The college draft also contributes to inter-team parity in the NFL, but it does so even more in the NBA. The impact of Major League Baseball's draft is less clear. It likely helps equalize talent there as well. But it takes longer to do so, as most MLB draftees first require a couple of years of seasoning in the minor leagues.

Other fans stressed their favorite sport's **strategic nature**:

[Baseball] ... always keeps me guessing and hypothesizing
what could happen next.
  – Texas woman, 21

[I like] the strategy, the battle of pitcher versus hitter,
the drama it can create.
  – 41 year-old New York man

Every pitch is a new possibility.
  – 31 year-old New Jersey woman

Trying to predict the plays . . . allows me to use my analytical skills.
  – 30 year-old African-American man from Illinois,
    referring to NFL football

[I] enjoy analyzing the offensive and defensive schemes.
  – Tennessee male football fan, 34

Teamwork is also cited for making their favorite sport engaging, mainly by fans of football:

[Football is] the ultimate team sport.
  – 60 year-old man from Louisiana

Football is all about teamwork and that's what I love.
  – Male, 30, from Florida

*Teamwork is a must [in the NFL], and to be good everyone must be
on the same page.*
  – Male, 58 from North Carolina

Not surprisingly, those who write about sports similarly stress how teamwork is critical in football. The teamwork required in football has been compared to the choreography of dance in Broadway musicals.[94]

Many fans—especially those whose favorite sport is baseball, but not *only* baseball fans—savor the **atmosphere of watching their favorite sport in person**:

I love going to the [baseball] stadium and being with the crowd, eating hot dogs and peanuts. It's the whole experience I enjoy.
  – 63 year-old Nevada man

[G]oing to [baseball] games live is always a fun thing to do.
  – Oregon female, 18

I now turn to other reasons for liking a sport besides its being engaging.

2. *Liking the sport because of a favorite team and/or to express hometown/local support or loyalty* ("Team/Place" - 20% of fans)

While fans of all four sports will sometimes mention their favorite team as a reason for liking the sport, this tendency is most common among baseball fans, more than one-quarter of whom referred to specific teams like the Braves, Yankees, Royals, White Sox, Tigers, Giants, and Red Sox as reasons why they like baseball the most.

Other respondents make it explicit that they like their favorite sport because it's a way of showing support for their local region (or state) or for the area where they grew up or lived previously, which hosts a team they follow. In that sense, it's an expression of hometown loyalty or pride.

Overall, one in every five fans describes liking their favorite sport at least partly because it derives from, or is influenced by, liking a team that plays the sport, typically a local team or one they grew up with. The prominence of this type of answer suggests prior attraction to a team (implying primacy of team over sport) is fairly common, perhaps even more so than the reverse, as conjectured in the opening chapter. Many fans probably fail to separate the two when thinking about their spectating preferences and practices. There is little reason to doubt that feelings toward the sport and team are mutually reinforcing.[95]

Here are examples of liking a sport because of a team or out of hometown pride:

> *I live in Texas but grew up in Boston. Like everyone who has Boston roots, I
> love my Red Sox. I keep up with how they are doing.*
> > – Texas woman, 60

> *Because we have our own hockey team—Tampa Bay Lightning!*
> > – Florida woman, 62

> *[I] live in Minnesota and the Vikings are here.
> Have to root for the local team.*
> > – 48 year-old Minnesota man

For one elderly fan in Ohio, anticipation of future success, possibly to vindicate years
of thwarted fandom, has been a life-sustaining activity: *I'm a Browns fan. I'm 83 years
old—and that's what's keeping me alive—that one day we'll win again.*

3. Liking the sport because it's my tradition, liking it for a long time, or I grew up with it ("My Tradition " – 11% of fans)

Some fans responded that they like their favorite sport because it is a tradition for
them, often a long tradition. Such comments are often expressed in the context
of fond memories of family and childhood. This too is particularly characteristic of
baseball fans.[96]

> *I've followed baseball since I was 9 in 1962. We had the Yankees and Mets,
> and Mickey Mantle was my favorite. I watched baseball - both Yankees and
> Mets - with my mother on a black and white TV. And also listened on my
> transistor radio.*
> > – New York woman, 62

> *Reminds me of my childhood when I watched baseball with my dad every
> Saturday.*
> > – Arkansas woman, 52

> *I've been watching baseball since 1947, and loved it then and love it now.*
> > – New York man, 76

> *I am a HUGE baseball fan. Love playing the game. Love coaching my sons
> as they play. Grew up watching the Tigers play. Watched my father and
> brothers play baseball and softball.*
> > – 42 year-old Indiana male

Michael Mandelbaum writes that baseball evokes childhood more powerfully than
other sports because it is played outside in summer, when kids can be carefree,
released from school-imposed discipline, constant parental supervision, and other

responsibilities and routines.[97]

I think Mandelbaum is on to something here. Watching (and playing) baseball outdoors in pleasant weather, unencumbered by school and family based restrictions, can only heighten nostalgic associations with the pre-eminent summertime sport. Furthermore, the closer connection of the "my tradition" theme to baseball (than to other sports) might also have something to do with baseball's longer schedule, making it more likely to become part of the fabric of one's daily life.

In my interview with Nancy, 74, a Cubs fan who lives in Chicago but grew up in southern Wisconsin, she vividly related a memory of watching the Cubs play at Wrigley Field one summer afternoon when she was young. What made the game memorable was her mother trusting her and her two sisters to make the 62-mile trip, which involved a train transfer, by themselves without adult supervision. She was 6 at the time; her sisters were 10 and 12. Nancy went on to marvel at how different things are now—how parents these days would never allow children of that age to make such a trip unaccompanied by an adult.

While nostalgic memories of growing up with the sport are most typical of baseball fans—in fact, it is one of the factors that most differentiates baseball fans from others—such sentiments were also expressed by fans of football and basketball (although seldom by hockey fans):

> I have always loved watching and playing basketball, even as a child.
> – 31 year-old African-American male in North Carolina

> Been a fan since high school. My dad loved it and taught me to enjoy it. My husband and I met at one [football game]
> – California woman, 65

> [Football has] been a part of me since youth. My parents were fans and passed it along to me, and I [to] my kids.
> – African-American male in Connecticut, 44

> [Basketball is] a sport I grew up watching most, with family.
> – 29 year-old African-American man from Illinois, Miami Heat fan

4. "Just like" – 10% of fans.

These are positive but typically vague, succinct responses not explaining why the sport is liked, "great", "interesting", "enjoyable", or "entertaining". They do not require illustration.

5. Fans whose favorite sport is based on family or social reasons ("Family/Social" – 8% of fans)

Sports spectating is often enjoyed in the company of family. It can be a simple shared interest or a treasured source of bonding in which family members share allegiance to the same team. Though less common, a friendly competition can arise in some families when different members support rival teams. Consistent with other research[98], women were more likely than men—about twice as likely—to give a family-oriented reason for why they like their favorite sport.

> *[Football is] something fun I get to do with my husband.*
>   – Wyoming woman, 30

> *[Baseball] is a sport that brings the family together. It has always been a tradition in my family to watch.*
>   – Pennsylvania woman, 51

> *[Football] is something my family bonds over.*
>   – 18 year-old Wisconsin male

> *It's the time my family comes together and we all have our favorite [NFL] team's jersey on and cheer for our teams.*
>   – African-American woman, 53, from New Jersey

In a poignant December 2015 story in *Sports Illustrated's The Cauldron*, Justin Wise, then an undergraduate at University of Oregon and sportswriter for the school's *Daily Emerald*, described the father-son bonding that occurs around talking sports:

> *When my father passed away, I feared I'd lost my biggest connection to being a fan. Instead, I learned the most precious thing about sports isn't the competition, but the conversation.*[99]

Apart from bolstering family ties, sports spectating is also a vehicle for non-family social interaction; for example, some Sports Fan Survey respondents commented that they like to watch their favorite sport in the company of friends, that one of the players is an acquaintance, or that they relish discussing players, teams, and outcomes. Regardless of the specific situation, about one in every twelve sports fans mentioned family or social reasons for liking their favorite sport.

NFL football games have become, or perhaps always have been, contests that fans like to enjoy with others. Viewing parties, especially but not solely on Super Bowl

Sunday, attract widespread participation. Part of the reason might be that football is ideally suited for television viewing because the TV screen can capture things happening simultaneously on different parts of the field.

Although comments about watching hockey, basketball, and baseball in the company of others are not absent, this social dimension is noticeably more prevalent among football fans.

> As I learned the sport [football] with my boyfriend. It became a great conversation topic after the game.
> – 20 year-old Hispanic woman in Oregon

> [Football is] a fun sport to watch, especially with friends.
> – 69 year-old Nebraska woman

> I enjoy watching the games with friends or at a bar. It is the social aspect that I enjoy. [Football] provides a sense of community that transcends SES [socio-economic status], education, ethnicity, etc. It's an easy way to make friends.
> – South Carolina male, 26

> I love tailgating and the social aspect [of football].
> – Illinois woman, 60

> I mostly watch [hockey] to hang out with friends who also enjoy it.
> – 20 year-old female from South Dakota.

When I asked Julie, who works for an investment company in Chicago, about the benefits of being a sports fan (in her case, a Blackhawks hockey fan), she told me how it has helped "bring me out with other people" (to counteract her shyness).

Manny, a 66 year-old Latino who works in retail in Texas, commented on how having a fan interest in sports can also be of value in one's work. The San Antonio Spurs basketball team are broadly popular in the region, possibly in part because they're the city's only major league sports team. A Spurs enthusiast since the team began playing in San Antonio in 1973, Manny related to me how the Spurs can be a natural conversation starter with customers whom he might not have much else in common. I cite this as an illustration of how being a fan can provide commercial benefits by facilitating socializing in a business context.

6. Being the favorite sport because I play it, or I played it when younger ("Played " - 6% of fans)

An easily understood reason for liking a sport is having been a participant in that sport.

Playing the sport or having played the sport when younger was the 6th most common reason cited for choosing it as one's favorite big4 sport. Some illustrations:

I played [basketball] all my life and love watching it.
   – 43 year-old white woman from Ohio

Baseball was the game I played most growing up, and always enjoyed watching it as well.
   – 58 year-old North Dakota man

[Hockey is] the game I grew up playing.
   – Texas man, 75

I like to watch NFL football because I am a former football player.
   – 58 year-old African-American male from Maryland

7. *Enjoying the rough, hard-hitting, sometimes violent play ("Physical" – 5% of fans)*

Some earlier comments illustrating the "engaging" theme hinted at the attraction of the physicality of the action on the field, court, or rink. While not particularly prevalent overall, responses that overtly referenced such reasons were placed in a separate category because of how dramatically fascination with the highly physical, hard-hitting nature of the games differentiates hockey and football fans from others. Some of the comments, like the quote that leads off this chapter, unabashedly reveal being attracted by the violence:

It's entertaining to watch big guys hit each other.
   – 22 year-old Michigan man who prefers football

[I like hockey] because it's a rough sport.
   – Woman from Tennessee, 45

[I like] the action, the skill, and the fights.
   – A 25 year-old female hockey fan from New Jersey

I like that it's a full-contact sport.
   – 28 year-old male football fan from Montana

I like the violence.
   – Texas football fan, 43 year-old male

Mandelbaum asserts that part of football's appeal derives from offering its audience a measure of violence, implying this is strategic on the part of the teams and TV networks. He compares this attraction to the gladiatorial contests of ancient Rome, the public hangings of early modern England, boxing in the past two centuries, and even to certain Hollywood movies of the present, while acknowledging that football is "a controlled and non-lethal version of [the violence]."[100]

Not everyone agrees violence is the, or even a, dominant attraction of football (or of other contests such as hockey). While acknowledging that violence plays a part, essayist Joseph Epstein prefers to distinguish between violence and roughness—the willingness of players to absorb rough blows and otherwise mix it up that draws some fans to watch. According to Epstein, emphasizing violence as the primary attraction is an exaggeration and falsely implies that "enthusiasm for sports among Americans is little more than a reflection of the national penchant for violence."[101]

8. References to liking participants in the sport, but not solely to their athletic prowess ("Players" – 3% of all fans; 7% of NBA fans)

This type of response is most characteristic of fans of NBA basketball, for whom this reason is at least twice as common. Starling is a 31 year-old African-American attorney in North Carolina. When I asked which is his favorite pro basketball team, he answered that, in contrast to football where he's a fan of the Dallas Cowboys (the team), in basketball he's more a fan of players than teams. The response underscores the appeal of individual players in the NBA.

These are examples of other responses in the "players" category:

> [NBA basketball is my favorite because of] LeBron.
> – 19 year-old African-American male in Ohio

> Stephen Curry is the next Michael Jordan.
> – Hispanic woman from Illinois, 41

> I get to watch my favorite [football] players from college
> go on into the pros.
> – Tennessee male, 23

> I love Bryce Harper on Washington Nationals team.
> – African-American woman in North Carolina, 61

9. I like the sport because it is easy to understand/follow. ("Easy to follow" – 3% of fans)

This unexpected type of response to the favorite sport query is most prevalent among Major League Baseball fans. It's also decidedly a more common type of answer given by women than men across all four sports.

In some cases, respondents' intended meaning of "easy" is ambiguous—it might reflect the slower pace of baseball (that it doesn't require constant attention)—but others might be referring to ability to follow what is happening on the field or even understanding the rules of the game.

> *It is what I grew up with and I understand the game.*
> – Georgia woman who likes Major League Baseball best, 57

> *I know the rules and I like the team.*
> – 53 year-old female baseball fan in Alabama

> *I like that basketball is fast paced and exciting. The rules are easy to understand.*
> – 41 year-old woman from Oregon

> *[Hockey] seems to have much less of a complicated rule set than football and baseball do, and it's easier for me to follow.*
> – Virginia woman, 32

10. I like the sport because its teams or players embody positive values or because the league or the teams do things to benefit the community ("Values"- 3% of fans)

This sentiment is more often expressed about Major League Baseball and NBA basketball. But value-based themes are not entirely missing from football fans' responses.[102]

> *[Baseball players'] sportsmanship is top notch, and they give a lot back to their communities.*
> – Minnesota woman, 35

> *Beautiful game [baseball], not a lot of problems like the NFL with domestic abuse.*
> – South Carolina male, 43

> *[The] whole family can enjoy [NBA basketball] - great role models, healthy lifestyle.*
> – 37 year-old Arkansas male

> *[The NFL] is ... very involved with communities and children.*
> – Idaho woman, 45

11. Baseball's slow(er) pace, longer season, and relative absence of violence ("Civil/Slower/Human Scale" – 3% of all big4 fans; 8% of baseball fans)

Baseball's leisurely, unhurried pace, offering spectators respite from the frantic rhythms of everyday life, and its lower level of physical impact and violence appeal to baseball fans. Comments falling into this category are almost exclusively limited to fans choosing baseball as their favorite sport.

Its more human scale appeals to some baseball fans:

> *Size does not matter.*
> – Hispanic male in Texas, 58

> *Small guys who can hit, run, throw, or defend at a position have a chance to play.*
> – 70 year-old man from Kansas

> *You don't have to be 6 foot 7 and weigh 300 pounds to play baseball.*
> – 65 year-old North Carolina man

> *It's a sport anyone can play.*
> – California woman, 64

Others prefer baseball because of its relative absence of violence:

> *I like the pace, and for the most part it's non-violent.*
> – 57 year-old African-American Maryland woman

> *[Baseball is] a sport where few players are mangled.*
> – Texas man, 77

> *Baseball is fun without the violence.*
> – Male, 68, from New York

And still others like baseball because of its long leisurely schedule or pace:

> *Baseball is life. I love the length of the season; [also,]the large number of games and the identity each team develops over the course of a season.*
> – 45 year-old Louisiana man

> *I like that it's a summer sport. It is … a slow-paced sport that is easy and relaxing.*
> – 38 year-old Connecticut man

> *The slower pace of it is charming.*
> – 21 year-old Texas female

> *You don't have to watch every play/pitch to keep up with the game [baseball]. Reading a book/newspaper while watching is perfectly OK.*
> – Male New Yorker, 72

In sharp contrast to how some baseball fans appreciate its long but leisurely season, some football fans said they *like* football's relatively abbreviated schedule because having only 16 regular season games enables viewers to watch each one with building anticipation for the seven days preceding the game.

> *Gives you something to look forward to once a week and not everyday.*
>   – African-American Louisiana man, 52

> *I like that [football] is played only once a week so you have the anticipation of waiting for the game. Plus the excitement of all the fanfare makes it a huge event.*
>   – 51 year-old New Hampshire woman

Writer Joe Queenan sees the once-a–week scheduling of football as advantageous to fans whose team wins, usually permitting them to savor the victory for a full week, which is not possible in sports with fuller, more compressed schedules. In baseball, "the afterglow of victory can be dissipated the following afternoon" or even "by the second half of a doubleheader."[103]

Recapping why fans like their favorite professional team sport

Sports fans offer many different reasons when asked what they like about watching their favorite professional team sport. As expected, the most common type of response, with baseball being a notable exception, is being sufficiently engaged (excited, interested, entertained) by what is happening during the game. This takes many different forms—liking or appreciating the action, intensity, competitiveness, drama, athleticism, strategy, or teamwork involved. Beyond this dominant assortment of mostly emotion-laden responses to the play of the game, less prevalent mentions are geographic or team-based reasons, the continuation of long-term evocative traditions or practices, social or familial reasons, having played the sport, the physicality of the game, and other, less commonly mentioned factors.

Consistent with the implications of George Carlin's stand-up routine comparing football and baseball, the analysis reveals meaningful differences between what motivates and appeals to fans of the two games—baseball fans being relatively less engaged by rapid continuous action and rough physicality, and more driven by deliberate one-on-one match-ups and intricate camouflaged strategies, being at the ballpark on a delightful summer day or evening; also by allegiance to team or place and fond memories of learning, watching, or playing the game when young.

Hockey fans are especially attracted to their game's constant action, fast pace, and physical contact. As for basketball fans, they are most inclined to mention specific players and, in contrast to football and baseball fans, players' athleticism.

A few final thoughts about why people today are attracted to sports

Chip Scarinzi offers an explanation why people like being sports fans, while not mentioned explicitly by fans in the survey, seems a deeper and more articulate encapsulation of the "engaging" theme:

> The act of cheering (or booing) a sports team provides a safe haven for people to connect with the peaks and valleys of the emotional spectrum ... allowing for the release of significantly raw and honest sensations that we otherwise hold back in our civilized workaday lives.[104]

No doubt, being a release valve for pent-up emotional energy accounts for some fans' attraction to sports. Although this wasn't a prominent theme in the survey responses, several fans I interviewed later in greater depth by telephone did mention how watching sports is a stress reliever for them and a welcome respite from the daily grind. Kelli, a Jacksonville Jaguars fan who lives in northern Florida, told me: "I'm sure that watching the games together on Sundays produces a release of tension that we all enjoy . . . That's a big part of it for me at least."

Joseph Epstein in *Masters of the Games* makes three compelling observations about what draws people to watch sports. One attraction is the desire to watch "the practice of a craft at a very high order, which is intrinsically interesting"—a reason expressed in a variety of ways by many respondents in our survey.

A second, perhaps more original reason put forth by Epstein is the unique authenticity of sport in today's society, unlike in most other realms of life, like "advertising, politics, business, and journalism," which makes it "greatly satisfying to watch."[105]

The third observation is the satisfaction of watching sports that derives from their special clarity. By this he means several things. First, the clarity that numbers bring—the statistics used to grade every aspect of performance. Clarity also refers to clarity of character. Epstein cites two examples—Dustin Pedroia of the Boston Red Sox and Joachim Noah of the Chicago Bulls [now playing for the New York Knicks]—"athletes who supplement reasonably high levels of ability with unreasonably high levels of courage and desire."[106]

The two latter appeals—authenticity and clarity—recall motivations noted in the previous chapter describing theories of fan attachment. Unlike the first attraction Epstein posits (the attraction of watching athletes perform at the highest level), authenticity and clarity go virtually unmentioned by respondents in the Sports Fan Survey. This might be because fans are not consciously aware of it possibly because these ideas are somewhat abstract and difficult to articulate.

Chapter 6:

National Popularity of Big4 Teams

The kick-ass Warriors! Holy cannoli, what a season!!!
– 40 year-old California woman and Golden State
Warriors fan describing why she likes NBA basketball

Having investigated sports fans' favorite big4 sports, we now turn to look at their favorite football, baseball, basketball, and hockey teams. While other indicators of team popularity are available, such as game attendance, road game attendance, television audience, franchise value, fan club membership, team paraphernalia sales, and total revenues, not until the Sports Fan Survey has a national sample of fans been asked to name their favorite professional team in each of the sports they follow.

Some of the resulting favorite team rankings might come as a surprise to readers, even to avid fans or close followers of the particular sport. But my objective is more ambitious than ranking the teams on national popularity simply to satisfy reader curiosity. It is also to account for some teams' disproportionate popularity—why certain teams elicit more fan appeal than others—beyond the obvious reason that some are located in larger markets—and why others evoke lower than expected enthusiasm. To address a core question posed at the outset, the purpose is, in other words, to analyze the rankings in the hope of uncovering factors apart from geographic proximity that help account for team followings.

My plan is to identify teams eliciting higher or lower than expected numbers of fans, and search for reasons that might help explain the disparities. The next two chapters also address the issue of team popularity, but in a different manner—by analyzing the answers given by fans when asked directly what they like about their favorite team and how their allegiance originated.[107] The macro level approach used here should complement—and possibly offer clues about—the individual level analyses which follow.

The number of each team's fans in the Sports Fan Survey should be approximately proportionate to the size of each team's geographic fan base—however that's defined, as metropolitan region, media market, state or cluster or adjacent states without teams, or whatever measure one chooses to use (I will use media market)—*if fans chose only teams in their market as their favorite.*[108] In other words, the rankings

Table 6.1: Favorite National Football League Team
(Base: fans who follow NFL football)

Team	Football Fans Selecting as Favorite Football Team	% of Football Fans Selecting as Favorite Football Team	Rank
Dallas Cowboys[110]	104	9.1	1
New England Patriots	84	7.4	2
Denver Broncos	78	6.9	3
Green Bay Packers	75	6.6	4
Pittsburgh Steelers	72	6.3	5
New York Giants	63	5.6	6
Chicago Bears	61	5.4	7
Seattle Seahawks	56	4.9	8
San Francisco 49ers	44	3.9	9
Washington Redskins	37	3.3	10
Philadelphia Eagles	37	3.3	10
Carolina Panthers	33	2.9	12
Indianapolis Colts	28	2.4	13
Atlanta Falcons	26	2.3	14
Cleveland Browns	25	2.2	15
Detroit Lions	25	2.2	15
New Orleans Saints	25	2.2	15
Oakland Raiders	24	2.1	18
Minnesota Vikings	22	2.0	19
San Diego Chargers	22	1.9	20
New York Jets	21	1.9	20
Arizona Cardinals	21	1.8	22
Miami Dolphins	21	1.8	22
Kansas City Chiefs	20	1.7	24
Houston Texans	19	1.7	24
Baltimore Ravens	17	1.5	26
Tampa Bay Buccaneers	16	1.4	27
Cincinnati Bengals	14	1.3	28
St. Louis/Los Angeles Rams	14	1.3	28
Buffalo Bills	12	1.1	30
Tennessee Titans	11	1.0	31
Jacksonville Jaguars	3	0.3	32
None	5	0.4	
TOTAL	1,136*	100%*	

* Small discrepancies may appear because the data are weighted and the numbers of fans are rounded to the nearest whole (the percentages to the nearest tenth).

should correspond to the relative size of these "natural" fan bases except when other factors besides "home team" or geographic proximity are significantly affecting team popularity.[109] (This logic obviously does not apply to Canadian teams, which are grayed out in the tables, because the book's focus is limited to U.S. sports fans.)

Because the inexactness of media market size as a measure of what I'm calling the "natural fan base," to be conservative I will examine only the extreme anomalies. There are indeed some obvious exceptions in the ranking tables shown below, in which teams score much higher or lower than the size of their geographic fan base suggests. It is these "anomalies" that should be instructive to consider. A close examination of the anomalies should point toward factors affecting team attachment *other than* geographic proximity.

Anomaly #1: Green Bay Packers. Ranked as the 4th most often chosen favorite team, selected by nearly 7% of NFL football fans, the Packers are located in the smallest market by far of any NFL team.[111] Two-thirds of those selecting them as their favorite team reside outside Wisconsin—from 24 other states as far away as Hawaii—giving them a truly national following. Something else besides proximity must explain their exceptional popularity. Some Packers fans in the Sports Fan Survey reported liking that the team is publicly owned, as fans can buy a piece of the organization. Far more likely, however, the main reason for the Packers being a fan favorite is their rich tradition, initiated by legendary coach Vince Lombardi, and their recent success, ranking 4th among NFL teams with 98 wins between 2005 and 2014[112]. The Packers rank as fans' 3rd *most favorite sports team overall*—the team fans would choose to watch and follow more than their respective favorites in the other big4 sports.[113]

Anomaly #2: Pittsburgh Steelers. The Steelers' unusually strong ranking (5th highest) surprised me as much as any other, with Pittsburgh being only the 20th largest television market hosting an NFL team. Well over half of the fans marking the Steelers as their favorite team (57%) live outside of Pennsylvania—a figure that would be higher if we excluded Pennsylvania fans living closer to Philadelphia than Pittsburgh and thus more naturally affiliated with the Eagles. The Steelers have won more games in the 2005-2014 period than any NFL football team other than the Patriots and the Colts, including two Super Bowls (six altogether), so success must be a major contributor to their popularity. I also speculate that some fans might identify with Pittsburgh as a gritty, industrial, working-class city which has modernized and diversified its local economy from being a struggling rust belt town. (The latter theme was, in fact, articulated in one of the in-depth telephone interviews by Tannis, a middle-age Pennsylvania woman and long-time Steelers fan.) In the overall favorite sport ranking—the team fans would choose if they could watch only one of their big4 sports favorites—the Steelers are 4th most often chosen. (As will be seen, disproportionate popularity also applies to Pittsburgh's other big4 teams.)

Anomaly #3: Denver Broncos. The Broncos are ranked 3rd in number of fans but located in the 18th largest media market. Their 2016 Super Bowl victory, featuring popular veteran quarterback Peyton Manning, playing his last game, likely contributed to their outsized popularity. They also have the 7th most NFL wins in the last ten years. The size of the Denver market probably underestimates their true fan base, as maps displaying where Broncos' fans live[114] have the most extensive territory (though lightly populated), almost certainly because Denver is the second most isolated NFL franchise location—the second most distant from any other team in the league (after Seattle). For that reason, Denver's strong popularity might be somewhat less of an anomaly than it at first appears to be. But even factoring in this consideration, the Broncos remain the favorite team of a much higher than expected number of football fans.

Anomaly #4: Carolina Panthers, Indianapolis Colts, and New Orleans Saints. These are three smaller market teams—ranking 22, 23, and 31, respectively, in size of markets with NFL teams—that out-perform in terms of being fan favorites, ranking 12, 13, and tied for 15th in popularity. In each case, recent success is the likely reason. The Colts have won more games in the past ten years than any team other than the Patriots and have made it to two Super Bowls; the Saints have the 10th highest number of wins and captured the Super Bowl in 2010; and the Panthers, who are fairly new to the NFL, won the AFC championship and appeared in the 2016 Super Bowl. In Cam Newton, the aforementioned Peyton Manning (who played many years for the Colts before moving to the Broncos), and Drew Brees, the teams also have had star quarterbacks liked by fans. The Saints might also be a sentimental favorite among some fans in the aftermath of Katrina, as suggested in several comments in the Sports Fan Survey.

Anomaly #5: New York Jets and Houston Texans. The relative *lack of popularity* of these teams represents the reverse anomaly—scoring fewer favorite votes among fans than their respective fan base populations would suggest. Two reasons for this underperformance come to mind—absence of success over the past decade, ranking 19th and 20th, respectively, in wins during 2005-2014, and their geographic closeness to well-regarded competitor NFL team (the Giants and the Cowboys). Also, the Jets and the Texans are more recent additions to the NFL than their respective geographic competitors, the Giants and Cowboys, which could also contribute to their under-performance, especially Houston's.

Coincidentally or not, the two NFL teams designated by the most fans as their favorite—the Dallas Cowboys and the New England Patriots—also happen to be the #1 and #2 most valuable NFL franchises in the league, according to *Forbes* magazine.[115] And, because success (popularity?) can also breed abhorrence, these same teams are now also the most *dis*liked by fans, with the Patriots finishing just ahead of the Cowboys in that unwelcome competition, based on a poll taken just before the 2017 Super Bowl.[116]

I now turn to a similar analysis of baseball teams, highlighting those generating far more or far fewer favorite selections than their natural fan base population would indicate.

Anomaly #1: Boston Red Sox. Almost 9% of baseball fans like the Red Sox best—a figure exceeded only by the New York Yankees. Anyone who follows major league baseball knows the Red Sox have an immense, enthusiastic tribe of supporters throughout the country, far exceeding the size or geographic scope of New England.[117] Nate Silver found that the Red Sox were the topic of more Google searches (using another indicator of popularity) than any baseball team except the Yankees—but *almost* as many as the Yankees, which has a much larger natural population to draw from. When relative market population is taken into account, the Red Sox have the greatest popularity of all baseball teams, in Silver's analysis.[118]

In my Sports Fan Survey, 55% of their followers live outside of the 6-state New England region. While the Red Sox's recent success likely has something to do with their popularity—they rank 5th among all MLB teams in the number of wins over the past 10 years (2006-2015) including two recent World Series championships (after a long hiatus)—other factors likely also help explain their outsized following. These might include the adoration of Fenway Park (the oldest MLB stadium), the sizable number of young fans temporarily living in New England during their college years, and the intensified sense of community or pride felt by fans living in a distinctive, somewhat isolated region of the country. For New Englanders, could it also have something to do with the Red Sox being associated with the coming of spring (and thawing temperatures) in a part of the country known for severe winters?[119]

Anomaly #2: St. Louis Cardinals. The Cardinals are another team that outperforms, given the size of its market. Operating from the 19th largest TV market with an MLB team, they tie for 6th in the number of baseball fans selecting them as their favorite.

Table 6.2: Favorite Major League Baseball Team
(Base: fans who follow Major League Baseball)

Team	Baseball Fans Selecting as Favorite Baseball Team	% of Baseball Fans Selecting as Favorite Baseball Team	Rank
New York Yankees	90	12.1	1
Boston Red Sox	67	8.9	2
Atlanta Braves	51	6.9	3
Chicago Cubs	49	6.5	4
Los Angeles Dodgers	41	5.4	5
St. Louis Cardinals	37	4.9	6
New York Mets	36	4.9	6
Detroit Tigers	27	3.6	8
Philadelphia Phillies	27	3.6	8
San Francisco Giants	27	3.6	8
Seattle Mariners	27	3.6	8
Pittsburgh Pirates	23	3.1	12
Texas Rangers	21	2.8	13
Los Angeles Angels	20	2.7	14
Kansas City Royals	20	2.6	15
Cleveland Indians	19	2.6	15
Chicago White Sox	18	2.4	17
Cincinnati Reds	18	2.4	17
Baltimore Orioles	17	2.3	19
Houston Astros	17	2.2	20
Minnesota Twins	16	2.2	20
Milwaukee Brewers	15	1.9	22
Arizona Diamondbacks	13	1.7	23
Oakland Athletics	10	1.3	24
Washington Nationals	10	1.3	24
Colorado Rockies	8	1.1	26
San Diego Padres	8	1.1	26
Tampa Bay Rays	7	0.9	28
Toronto Blue Jays	4	0.6	29
Miami Marlins	3	0.4	30
None	3	0.4	
TOTAL	749*	100%*	

* Small discrepancies may appear because the data are weighted and the numbers of fans are rounded to the nearest whole (the percentages to the nearest tenth).

The Cardinals are the 3rd most successful team in MLB based on their number of wins in the past ten years, a perpetual play-off contender, and a three-time World Series contestant in the past decade, winning twice. The Cards rank 4th in Google searches, and 2nd only to the Red Sox in searches relative to the size of their market.[120] Like other smaller-market outperformers (the Pittsburgh Pirates are a good example), the Cardinals have a storied tradition that goes beyond on-the-field success and helps capture the loyalties of fans outside their natural market. (Almost half choosing them reside outside of Missouri.) Perhaps their attractive trademark uniforms, featuring a bright red cardinal perched upon a baseball bat, which I've always admired, has something to do with their appeal.

Anomaly #3: Pittsburgh Pirates and Kansas City Royals. The Pirates and Royals are two more teams with a greater number of favorite selections than their local area population would suggest, ranking 12th and tied for 15th in the survey, but located in the 20th and 23rd largest markets having a baseball team. The Pirates, but not the Royals, also score high in Google searches relative to "natural" fan base. Although both teams have been in the play-offs recently (the Royals having made it to the World Series in 2014 and 2015), this alone would not seem to account for their better than expected popularity, especially for the Pirates. In numbers of wins over the past ten years, both have poor records, ranking 26th (Pirates) and 27th (Royals). It is difficult to come up with a plausible reason for these teams' outperformance, except in the case of the Pirates—referring to Pittsburgh's reputation as a great sports town—which rings true but only begs the question of why.

Anomaly #4: Chicago White Sox, Houston Astros, and Washington Nationals. These three teams all underperform. Each is located in a heavily populated area (Chicago is the 3rd largest TV market, Houston is the 10th, and Washington is the 9th) but rank 17th (tied), 20th, and 24th, respectively, as baseball fans' favorite teams. The Nationals and Astros also rank near the bottom in Nate Silver's measure of popularity (number of Google searches relative to TV market size). All three are in the bottom half of teams with the most wins in the past ten years. The White Sox and the Nationals each have had to split at least part of their proximate fan base with another team (the Cubs and Orioles), somewhat mitigating those teams underperformance. Being relatively new to the Washington area—the franchise moved from Montreal in 2005—the Nationals also might not have had enough time yet to build strong fan attachments.

I move next to teams in the National Basketball Association teams.

Anomaly #1: Los Angeles Lakers. Coming as a surprise, the Lakers lead all NBA

Table 6.3: Favorite National Basketball Association Team
(Base: fans who follow NBA basketball)

Team	Basketball Fans Selecting as Favorite Basketball Team	% of Basketball Fans Selecting as Favorite Basketball Team	Rank
Los Angeles Lakers	77	11.8	1
Chicago Bulls	68	10.4	2
Golden State Warriors	57	8.8	3
Boston Celtics	55	8.4	4
Cleveland Cavaliers	52	7.9	5
San Antonio Spurs	41	6.3	6
Miami Heat	37	5.7	7
New York Knicks	33	5.1	8
Dallas Mavericks	23	3.5	9
Los Angeles Clippers	19	2.9	10
Detroit Pistons	18	2.7	11
Washington Wizards	17	2.7	12
Houston Rockets	14	2.1	13
Philadelphia 76ers	14	2.1	13
Oklahoma City Thunder	13	2.0	15
Sacramento Kings	12	1.8	16
Indiana Pacers	11	1.7	17
Orlando Magic	10	1.5	18
Phoenix Suns	10	1.5	18
Atlanta Hawks	9	1.4	20
Milwaukee Bucks	8	1.3	21
Charlotte Hornets	7	1.1	22
Portland Trailblazers	7	1.1	22
Denver Nuggets	6	0.9	24
New Orleans Pelicans	6	0.9	24
Utah Jazz	5	0.8	26
Minnesota Timberwolves	5	0.8	26
Memphis Grizzlies	5	0.8	26
Brooklyn Nets	5	0.7	29
Toronto Raptors	0	0.0	30
None	8	1.2	
TOTAL	652*	100%*	

* Small discrepancies may appear because the data are weighted and the numbers of fans are rounded to the nearest whole (the percentages to the nearest tenth).

teams as a fan favorite. While Los Angeles is the 2nd largest TV market in the country, the Lakers have had to share it with the Clippers. Moreover, although they have had one of the league's biggest stars in Kobe Bryant, the Lakers haven't enjoyed much success lately. For those two reasons, I categorize their highest popularity ranking as a different sort of anomaly. More than half of Laker fans reside outside of California. It might be that the Lakers' popularity partly reflects the past glory of the Magic Johnson and Kareem Abdul-Jabbar years.

> The Thunder are a great example of how the arrival of a major league franchise in a city that had never had one can generate immense excitement. Indeed, it can be the stimulus for civic revitalization in a psychological way, transcending whatever economic benefits the team provides. Karla, an OKC fan in her mid-50s who lives just outside Oklahoma City recounted how anyone interested in sports immediately became a follower of the Thunder when they arrived. Even non-fans appreciate having a professional team in the city..

Anomaly #2: Cleveland Cavaliers. Situated in only the 15th largest media market with an NBA team, they have the 5th largest number of fans across the country. The Cavs made it to the championship series the past three years against the resurgent and powerful Golden State Warriors, and won the crown in 2016, but not until after most of the Sports Fan Survey was completed, so I did not expect them to command such a large following. One likely reason is the popularity of Cavs' superstar LeBron James, mentioned by nine of the 21 Cleveland fans as a reason picking the Cavaliers as their overall favorite big4 sports team.[121] James's triumphant return to Cleveland after leaving for glitzy Miami was also a great story. A majority of Cavalier fans live outside of Ohio.

Anomaly #3: San Antonio Spurs and Oklahoma City Thunder. These two teams, from even smaller markets having an NBA team (22nd and 23rd largest), also outperform as fan favorites, being ranked 6th and 15th in popularity. Both teams have enjoyed great success, with winning percentages exceeding 60%, although Oklahoma City has hosted its team only since 2008. The Spurs are known for their team play and the solid organization, led by head coach Gregg Popovich. Over half of the Spurs' fans live outside of Texas. Tim Duncan, recently retired, will probably be in the NBA Hall of Fame sometime soon, but Duncan does not approach the celebrity status and drawing power of LeBron James. The Thunder's former star, Kevin Durant (now with

Table 6.4: Favorite National Hockey League Team
(Base: fans who follow NHL hockey)

Team	Hockey Fans Selecting as Favorite Hockey Team	% of Hockey Fans Selecting as Favorite Hockey Team	Rank
Chicago Blackhawks	62	15.6	1
Detroit Red Wings	35	8.9	2
Pittsburgh Penguins	30	7.7	3
Boston Bruins	29	7.3	4
New York Rangers	29	7.3	4
Philadelphia Flyers	20	5.1	6
Los Angeles Kings	19	4.8	7
St. Louis Blues	16	4.1	8
Colorado Avalanche	14	3.5	9
Tampa Bay Lightning	14	3.5	9
Dallas Stars	12	3.1	11
San Jose Sharks	11	2.9	12
Anaheim Ducks	11	2.7	13
Minnesota Wild	9	2.3	14
Washington Capitals	8	2.1	15
Arizona Coyotes	7	1.8	16
Buffalo Sabres	7	1.7	17
New Jersey Devils	7	1.7	17
New York Islanders	7	1.7	17
Columbus Blue Jackets	6	1.6	20
Nashville Predators	6	1.6	20
Florida Panthers	5	1.4	22
Toronto Maple Leafs	5	1.3	23
Vancouver Canucks	5	1.3	23
Montreal Canadiens	5	1.2	25
Carolina Hurricanes	5	1.2	25
Calgary Flames	2	0.5	27
Edmonton Oilers	2	0.5	27
Ottawa Senators	0	0.0	29
Winnipeg Jets	0	0.0	29
None	7	1.7	
TOTAL	395*	100%*	

* Small discrepancies may appear because the data are weighted and the numbers of fans are rounded to the nearest whole (the percentages to the nearest tenth).

the Warriors but who played for the Thunder when the survey was taken) stands closer to James as one of the league's most popular superstars and, therefore, probably attracted some additional fans to the Thunder.

Anomaly #4: Atlanta Hawks and Brooklyn Nets. The Hawks and Nets are distinct underperformers in terms of popularity relative to the size of their markets, even given that the Nets, ranked near the bottom in popularity, have to share the New York market, by far the nation's largest, with the New York Knicks. Atlanta is the 8th largest market, but the Hawks garner only the 20th most fans. The Nets' poor record of late no doubt contributes to their low popularity. Perhaps more paramount, having moved from New Jersey as recently as 2012, they have had only a brief period to build a fan base as a Brooklyn-based team. Neither team has had a player during the last several years approaching the star status of Kobe Bryant, LeBron James, or Steph Curry.

Lastly we take a look at the NHL's American hockey teams.

Anomaly #1: The Detroit Red Wings. Number 2 in the number of U.S. fans and number 9 in market size of U.S. teams with NHL teams, the Red Wings' outsized popularity warrants examination, but no plausible explanations spring to mind other than their consistent successful record, with the 3rd most wins in the last ten years, including a Stanley Cup in 2008.

Anomaly #2: The Pittsburgh Penguins. Playing in the 16th largest market with an NHL team, the Penguins have the 3rd most fans. Once again, their success very probably contributes to their outperformance. They have the most wins of any NHL team in the past decade, with three Stanley Cup championships including in 2016, at the height of the Sports Fan Survey data collection. They also feature several of the league's most exciting veteran stars in forwards Sidney Crosby and Evgeni Malkin.

Anomaly #3: The St. Louis Blues and Colorado Avalanche. These two teams also enjoy more popularity than their market size would indicate. While the Blues have the 10th best past-decade record—which could help explain their disproportionate number of fans—the same cannot be said for the Avalanche, which ranks 20th in victories. As noted above when discussing the Broncos, Denver's location, which is relatively isolated from other teams, gives them a true territorial fan base larger than its media market size suggests.

Anomaly #4: New York Islanders and Florida Panthers. These two are underperformers relative to their market size, even allowing for the Islanders having to share their market with the Rangers (also partly with the New Jersey Devils). To a lesser extent, the Panthers have to share part of their market with the Tampa Bay Lightning. The Islanders have the 7th worst record in the NHL over the past ten years, and the Panthers have the 4th worst record. Apart from the Panthers being the southernmost team in the NHL (Hockey tends to be more prominent in northern climes), I can conjure no other plausible reasons for these teams' lower than expected popularity.

Take-aways: factors explaining team attachments beyond residential proximity

As examined, some teams in each of the big4 sports attract more fans than expected under the assumption that *teams draw most of their fans from their geographic fan base*. The above analysis has been conservative in the sense of highlighting only teams whose fan size ranking is sharply different from their market size rank. Even so, more than a few "discrepant" cases were identified. Many of those cases could be explained by the team's having a very strong or very poor record of success. In a few cases, the team's popularity was attributed to popular star players. Another likely factor helping to account for team popularity in some cases (inversely) is insufficient tenure in the current location—not having had a minimum number of years playing in its current city to develop firm fan allegiances. As in other emotional relationships, the attachment between a team and its fans often takes time to solidify. Lastly, the distance from competitor teams should also independently impact the numbers of fans some teams will generate, if only modestly in some cases.

The next two chapters examine a closely related pair of questions—why fans like their overall favorite team and how that attachment originated—by asking them directly.

Chapter 7:

Choosing and Sticking with a Favorite Team, Part 1: The "Home Team" Effect and Geographic Proximity

My fondest memories of my father were centered around his love of baseball and his hometown of Houston. I guess it was natural for me to pick up the mantle of my hometown heroes!!
– Texas man, describing what contributed to his becoming an Astros fan

The prior chapter's analysis hinted that team success, star/celebrity players, a team's tenure in the city or region it represents, and existence of nearby competitor teams are additional factors beyond geographic proximity that help account for team attachments.

In this chapter and the next, I present answers from Sports Fan Survey respondents that bear on the precursors of team allegiance from a different angle—asking them directly why they like being a fan and how they originally came to choose their favorite team. I rely on two complementary approaches—(1) survey queries asking fans to answer those questions in their own words, and (2) checklists of plausible reasons describing why they chose their team and what maintains their interest.[122] This chapter also relies on a third piece of information—where fans lived when the chosen team first became their favorite.

The current chapter concentrates on the main reason why fans become and stay attached to a particular team—residential proximity (or "home team effect" – I use the terms interchangeably). Why it is the main factor, although far from the only factor, will soon be elaborated. The next chapter examines the importance of other elements that help explain fans' initial choice of a team or sustain their interest in it. Together, these sections provide a comprehensive inventory of reasons and motivations unlike anything previously compiled.

Overall favorite teams of U.S. sports fans

The data reviewed in this chapter and the next refer to fans' overall favorite team. To recall how that was determined, the Sports Fan Survey first asked respondents to choose their favorite team in each of the big4 sports they watch and follow; then, to designate which *one* of those teams is their overall favorite—their *most favorite of all to watch and follow?*[123]

Table 7.1: Top 25 Most Selected Overall Favorite Teams
(Fans could select only one team across the big4 sports as their overall favorite.)

	Sport	Number of Fans Choosing (%)		Rank
Dallas Cowboys	football	73	(5.6%)	1
New England Patriots	football	70	(5.4%)	2
Green Bay Packers	football	62	(4.7%)	3
Pittsburgh Steelers	football	60	(4.6%)	4
Denver Broncos	football	56	(4.3%)	5
New York Yankees	baseball	51	(3.9%)	6
Seattle Seahawks	football	45	(3.4%)	7
Chicago Bears	football	35	(2.7%)	8
New York Giants	football	34	(2.6%)	9
Washington Redskins	football	30	(2.3%)	10
Los Angeles Lakers	basketball	28	(2.2%)	11
Carolina Panthers	football	25	(1.9%)	12
San Francisco 49ers	football	24	(1.9%)	13
Atlanta Falcons	football	23	(1.8%)	14
Philadelphia Eagles	football	22	(1.7%)	15
New Orleans Saints	football	22	(1.7%)	15
Boston Red Sox	baseball	21	(1.6%)	17
Indianapolis Colts	football	21	(1.6%)	17
Golden State Warriors	basketball	21	(1.6%)	17
Cleveland Cavaliers	basketball	19	(1.5%)	20
Chicago Blackhawks	hockey	19	(1.5%)	20
Chicago Cubs	baseball	18	(1.4%)	22
San Diego Chargers	football	18	(1.4%)	22
Los Angeles Dodgers	baseball	18	(1.4%)	22
St. Louis Cardinals	baseball	18	(1.3%)	25
TOTAL		833*	(64%)*	

* Small discrepancies may appear because the data are weighted and the numbers of fans are rounded to the nearest whole (the percentages to the nearest tenth).

Table 7.1 displays the top 26 overall most favorite teams chosen by respondents:

Consistent with professional football being the most popular sport, NFL teams dominate this list, taking nine of the top ten positions and 17 of the top 25. In baseball, the Yankees (#6), the Red Sox (tied for #17), and the Cubs, Dodgers, and Cardinals (tied for #22) make the list. In basketball, the Lakers (#11), the Warriors (tied for #17) and the Cavaliers (tied for #20) were selected often enough to be in the top 25 overall favorites. Only one hockey team made the top 25 favorite teams—the Chicago Blackhawks (tied for #20).

Altogether, these top 25 teams account for 64% of the favorites chosen by the sports fans surveyed. Among all fans, 61% selected an NFL team as their overall favorite, 19% chose a Major League Baseball team as their overall favorite, 13% picked an NBA basketball team, and 7% selected an NHL hockey team. (Across the big4 sports, there are 122 teams in all—113 if the nine Canadian teams are excluded, seven of those being hockey teams.)

How many fans have lived closer to their favorite team than to a competitor?

We begin by calculating how many sports fans have chosen a favorite team that is now or was previously their home team or, if there is no team in their city or region, the geographically closest team. If, for example, the fan's overall favorite team is the Buffalo Bills, for the Bills to be considered that fan's home (closest) team, the fan must reside nearer to Buffalo than to any other NFL team's home location. If they happen to live a few miles closer to Cleveland or to Pittsburgh than to Buffalo (Orchard Park to be exact, where the Bills play in suburban Buffalo), then for this analysis that Bills fan would not be considered having chosen the home team as his or her favorite.[124][125]

There is also a distinction between current home team and former home team, if the fan has ever relocated closer to a different team *in that sport*. The Sports Fan Survey asked whether the favorite team:

1. was the closest [SPORT OF FAVORITE TEAM] team to where the fan lived at least part of the time as a child or teenager;

2. is the closest [SPORT OF FAVORITE TEAM] team to where the fan lives now; and if no to 1 and 2:

3. if the team became the fan's favorite [SPORT OF FAVORITE TEAM] team when the fan lived somewhere else. (This refers to a time in between now and when the fan was a child or teenager.)

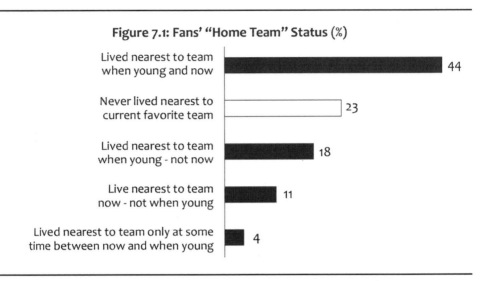

Figure 7.1: Fans' "Home Team" Status (%)

Lived nearest to team when young and now — 44

Never lived nearest to current favorite team — 23

Lived nearest to team when young - not now — 18

Live nearest to team now - not when young — 11

Lived nearest to team only at some time between now and when young — 4

Figure 7.1 shows that the largest segment of fans (44%) lived closest to their favorite team at least part of the time when they were a child or teenager, and still live closest to that team. Another 18% have retained the home team of their youth as their favorite, but now live closer to a different team in that sport. Only four percent have retained the home team of a previous residential location between their childhood/teenage years and now. And 11% of fans have a favorite team that's the home team of where they live now but wasn't the home team of where they lived when young.

So 77% of fans (the sum of the black bars) have at some period lived in a place closer to their current favorite team than to any competitor, leaving 23% of fans who have never lived in a location closest to their current favorite. This finding represents hard evidence supporting the conventional view of the dominant importance of "home team effect" (or residential proximity) in team attachments.

The contrast between the 44% + 11% = 55% who currently reside in a location nearest to their favorite team and the 44% + 18% = 62% who lived nearest to their current home team when young is interesting in itself, as it suggests early-life attachments might be slightly stronger than later ones. Moving forward, we will not maintain the distinction between current home team and prior home team except to revisit its meaning briefly in Chapter 9, when we look at fans whose favorite team has changed.

Are the 77% different from the 23%?

In some ways, yes, those who lived closest to their current favorite at some point in their life display different characteristics than those who never have (See Table 7.2). Fans whose favorite team plays hockey (or baseball, to a slightly lesser degree) are most likely to say they've lived closer to their current favorite team. Basketball fans are least likely to say they've lived closer to their favorite team than to another NBA team. Football fans fall in between. This moderate distinctiveness of basketball fans might be because, as noted earlier and as will be further documented, NBA basketball is the most individualistic, player dominated sport. The attraction to particular star players could override residential proximity as a key factor in team preference.

Table 7.2: Fans Who Have at Some Time Lived Closer to their Current Favorite Than to Another Team in the Same Sport (%)

Football is favorite	75
Baseball is favorite	82
Basketball is favorite	70
Hockey is favorite	85
African-American	64
Non African-American	79
Northeast	81
Midwest	80
South	69
West	80
18-29	72
30-44	75
45-59	75
60+	84

It could also be because fans choosing an NBA team as their favorite overall are disproportionately African-Americans, who as a group are less likely than non African-Americans to have lived most proximate to their favorite team (Table 7.1). If indeed they are less residentially mobile than others—perhaps due to having lower incomes, on average, and possibly also because they are more likely to encounter housing discrimination—lower mobility would afford African-Americans fewer opportunities to have lived near their favorite team at some point. Without a much larger sample, it's not possible to know whether it's race or something unique about being a basketball fan that's the main source of the contrast.

Fans in the South are also more likely than fans in other regions to have a favorite team in a location other than geographically proximate to where they've lived. This could be a result of fewer professional sports teams located in the South or fewer teams in the South of long-standing.

The last and potentially most intriguing distinction refers to age differences: The oldest segment of fans (60+) are more likely than their younger counterparts to have lived geographically proximate to their favorite team at some point in their lives. It could be that these older fans are simply more locally oriented. Alternatively, it might be that because they're older they have lived in more locations, on average, and so, have had more chances to live close to their chosen team at some time.

The latter interpretation is less likely, as the correlation across the four age segments is weak, showing only minor differences below age 60 (Table 7.1). If the age contrast uncovered were more a function of having lived in a greater number of locations, we would observe a sharper and more regular increase with increasing age. It is more likely that a cut-point exists in age spectrum of the population, in which fans who are in the oldest age segment have been more driven by local loyalties than younger fans, or for whatever reason might have found it harder to develop/pursue a more distant team. I return shortly to consider the meaning of this contrast and its intriguing implications.

Reasons fans originally chose their favorite team

When fans were asked directly in the survey why they initially chose their favorite team rather than some competitor, the number one theme in respondents' answers was *geographic proximity or to show support for one's city/state/region.* Fully forty-one percent of the answers fans wrote in their own words are captured by this theme.[126] These are some illustrations:

A 22 year-old Detroit Lions fan wrote:
   I lived in Detroit so I feel it was natural to root for the home team.[127]

A California woman, 68, responded:
   I chose them [the Denver Broncos] because I was born in Denver.

An 49 year-old Hispanic man in Texas wrote:
   It's simple, they [the Dallas Mavericks] play in my home state.

A 24 year-old Missouri male hockey fan explained:
   *They [the St. Louis Blues] are the closest to a hometown
   team that I have.*

A female Cowboys fan living in the state of Washington, 32, loudly proclaimed:
   I'M A LOYAL TEXAN , even if I reside elsewhere. My "home" is TEXAS.

Fans were also presented with a list of 14 reasons and asked to mark those that were contributing factors in their team selection. Over half (53%) marked *They were my home team* as a reason affecting their choice—more than any other item in the list. Altogether, 61% either referenced the *home team/residential proximity* theme when answering in their own words OR marked *They were my home team* from the list of reasons presented.

What sports fans like about being fans of their favorite team

As another angle on why big4 team fans watch and follow their favorite team, we used a similar approach to inquire what they *currently* like about that team. What specifically is it that sustains their interest as a fan?

Once again, the most common theme emerging from the answers to the open-ended question was *liking the chosen team because it is (or was) the fan's home team*, or *to support a city/region/state they like* (almost invariably their current location), or *because the team supports that geographic entity.*

For example, a Los Angeles Dodgers fan answered he likes being a fan because "It's part of being a native of L.A." An Arizona man wrote he likes the Arizona Cardinals "because they represent our state." An elderly football fan in Iowa wrote "The Chicago Bears are a local [team], close to Iowa, so I consider it a home team."

Rooting for a team from a beloved city or region where the fan used to reside can be a way of maintaining a connection with that area. Jolene, a 34 year-old woman now living in a town southeast of Tucson, Arizona, grew up a two hour drive from Seattle and misses much about life in Washington, including the water and trees. She remains an avid Seahawks fan, and continues to maintain a milder interest in the Mariners, in part because the teams evoke pleasant memories of her former residence.

Although home team/geographic proximity is not quite as important in sustaining fans' interest in their chosen team as it is for the fan's initial selection of that team, it is nevertheless a highly influential consideration at both stages.

The curious connection between age and the home team/proximity factor

Above we identified a correlation between older age and having lived in an area closest to one's favorite team. Specifically, only 16% of sports fans 60 and older had never resided in a place closest to their favorite team, compared to 26% of younger fans—an unlikely difference by chance. This implies geographic proximity is a greater factor in team selection among fans 60+ than among younger fans.

Responses to why fans originally chose their favorite big4 team and what they currently like about the team are also correlated with age. Fully 61% of fans 60 and older answered the first question by indicating that being the current or former "home team" (geographic proximity) was a factor in their choice of a favorite team, while far fewer younger fans (35%) gave that answer—a stunning contrast.

Similarly, 67% of this oldest fan segment marked *the team was my home team* from the list of reasons presented, compared to 48% of fans younger than 60. In response to what fans *currently* like about their favorite team, 35% of the 60+ age fans replied one thing they like is that the team is/was my home team, compared to 25% among younger fans. While this contrast is not as dramatic, it is nevertheless significant and consistent.

So, on all relevant measures seniors exhibit a more local orientation in team preferences than younger sports fans. The pattern applies to a modest degree across the age spectrum, but the main break point dividing the segments seems to be around age 60.

It is hard to come up with an obvious interpretation for this persistent contrast, but one possibility does spring to mind—different orientations toward modern electronic technology. If younger fans are more adept at, or comfortable with, new technologies that make it easier to watch games of non-local teams and to follow their progress, this could account for the difference. If there's any validity to this explanation, then we can expect local loyalties might continue to shrink as the population ages and, perhaps also, as technological advances continue to facilitate distant allegiances. This admittedly speculative line of thinking might be considered a country-based version of some of the same forces contributing to globalization.

Why do so many fans cheer for the local/nearby team?

Consistent with popular perceptions, residential proximity is a prevalent reason for choosing, and for liking, a favorite team. If more evidence is needed, the next chapter will show it clearly outdistances other causes of team attachment.

There are several plausible reasons why location should matter. First is accessibility: It is simply easier to follow a local (or nearby) team—easier to attend games in person; easier to watch games on television without an expensive supplemental cable subscription; and easier to be exposed to available media news and commentary by reporters, bloggers, talk shows, and team representatives. As Isaac, a 58 year-old from Akron, Ohio responded when I asked why he's a Cleveland Browns fan, "it's more convenient to root for the local team."

A second reason is the social environment: The local/closest team has numerous other followers who are part of a fan's family or network of friends, live in the neighborhood, or can be counted among acquaintances at work. Partly because of social pressures, most find it more comfortable rooting for the same team as others nearby, rather than allying with the opposition. In response to my question asking why Pittsburghers seem to be especially strong supporters of their hometown teams, Matt, 41, a Penguins fan in Erie, PA explained: "If you live in the area and you're not a supporter, you're pretty much an outcast." Apart from community pressure, following the local favorite(s) also can simply facilitate social intercourse.

Third, we tend to identify with institutions that are proximate and familiar. For example, residents of the metropolitan Atlanta who are proud of their city or region are likely to embrace the Atlanta Falcons (and the Braves and the Hawks) because they represent that region, especially during periods of team success, which adds stature to the region. Speaking from personal experience, my affection for the Twin Cities region that developed when I lived there as a graduate student surely contributed to my becoming a strong fan of the Twins in baseball and the Vikings in football.

Kelli in Ohio, 44, is a hockey fan who supports the Columbus Blue Jackets, partly "because they do a lot for the community—visiting children in hospitals, and so forth." She is one of many examples I could cite illustrating how civic pride often translates into support for the local favorite. (As a side note, the data I've compiled suggests this motivation might be more pronounced in intermediate and smaller size cities with only one professional team, such as Columbus, Oklahoma City, Sacramento, Memphis, Jacksonville, and Green Bay than in places like New York, Los Angeles, and Chicago.)

Summary

Considerable evidence from the survey supports the widespread (some would say, intuitive) view that sports fans most often decide to cheer for their current or former home team, or if there is/was no home team, the closest team. Beyond the survey evidence presented, several compelling reasons help us understand why this makes sense.

But "most often" does not equal "always." We found that nearly one-quarter of big4 team fans have made a selection that is NOT their current or former geographically proximate team, choosing instead to watch and follow one that's more distant. And far from all fans cited a home/closest team preference as a reason when asked why they chose their favorite team.

Certain identifiable segments of fans are less likely than others to choose a favorite team because of geographic proximity. This includes fans whose overall favorite is an NBA team, African-Americans, fans residing in the South and, most unexpectedly, sports fans not yet 60. If my interpretation of this age contrast is even partly valid—that younger fans use new technologies more than older fans, making it easier to follow non-local teams—then we might expect residential proximity to fade as a source of sports team attachments, if the process hasn't already begun.

The next chapter describes other reasons fans select a particular team as their favorite and why they continue to favor that team, and it illustrates the broad range of considerations motivating sports fans, some of them quite novel.

Chapter 8:

Choosing and Sticking With a Favorite Team, Part II: Other Factors Besides "Home Team"/Geographic Proximity

Most of my friends were [Detroit] Red Wings fans, and seeing them get excited about games did the same for me.
– 19 year-old Virginia female

I earlier described three models of possible relevance to sports fans' allegiances—the analogy to religious practices, secular quest for community, and identity theory. These models suggest specific, testable reasons why fans become and remain attached to particular teams, such as influence of family members and friends, desire for social connection/community, excitement or pleasure derived from watching the games, identification with certain players or coaches, team success, laudatory behavior, and the need to enhance self-esteem.

The reason that usually comes to mind first—supporting the home team or nearest team---could itself be related to desire for fellowship or community with fellow fans in the local area. Choosing to root for the home team or geographically closest team was separately addressed in the previous chapter and shown to be extensive. Two charts presented below validate it as the most important factor, based on how often fans mention it. However, it is not the only reason fans choose to cheer for a particular team, and sometimes not the primary factor. The other reasons and motivations are examined here. Like desire for social acceptance, some of these other reasons and motivations, overlap with rooting for the home team or nearest team (accessibility and long-time tradition, for instance), making it difficult to achieve a clean distinction.

We rely on two of the same types of data as in Chapter 7—themes extracted from fans' own words and prepared lists of reasons the respondents could mark. Both speak to the inter-related questions we want to address—(1) why fans originally chose their favorite team rather than some competitor and (2) why they like being a fan, that is, what they currently like about the team.

Describing the main factors affecting team preference and appeal

Table 8.1 provides a summary of the most often expressed themes—the reasons

Table 8.1: Reasons Why Fans Chose Their Favorite Team and What They Like About Being a Fan of the Team
(Expressed in written responses to the open-ended questions)

Theme/ Reason	Description
Home team/ geographical proximity*	Current home team or nearest team. Home or nearest team of former residence. To support city or state. Team promotes the city/region.
Family	Parent, spouse, or other family member was a fan or was influential in becoming a fan of the team. Enjoys watching games with family.
My (long) tradition	Have liked team for a long time or always liked. Memories watching/following team when young.
Engaging	Games are exciting, dramatic, suspenseful, competitive, intense, strategic, action packed, fast-paced, physical/tough; or specific expertise noted.
Players	Current players mentioned. Like following players' development. Know some of the players.
Other fans & friends (social)	One or more friends like(d) the team. Became a fan to enjoy watching/following with friends.
Team's success	Team wins a lot, has had strong recent record.
Team's/ players' values	Does good things for the community. Charitable. Displays positive values. Team diversity/tolerance. Treats fans well. Fosters broad sense of community.
Organization/ management	Like(d) coaches/owners/announcers. Classy/professional organization. Makes good decisions. Team is publicly owned (Green Bay Packers).
History	Like(d) team's strong reputation, legacy, tradition (not just current success). Former players mentioned.
Memorable first game or other game	Became favorite because saw them play first or because of a particular influential game.
Branding	Like(d) uniforms, colors, logo, mascot, nickname; good promotions.
Like(d) sport or play(ed) sport	Like(d) being a fan because like the sport; play or played that sport.
Accessible	Easy to watch/follow because team's location, access to games on TV.
Local norms	Strong community sentiment/pressure to be a fan.

* This reason was thoroughly addressed in the previous chapter.

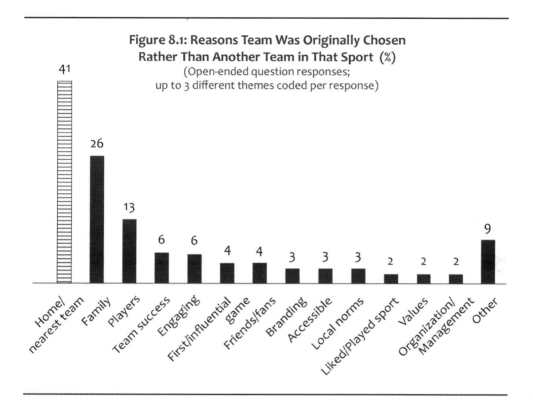

Figure 8.1: Reasons Team Was Originally Chosen Rather Than Another Team in That Sport (%)
(Open-ended question responses; up to 3 different themes coded per response)

inferred from fans' answers to why they chose their preferred team and why they like them now.

Figure 8.1 provides a visual depiction of the incidence of the various themes expressed in fans' answers to the open-ended question asking *why fans originally chose their favorite team to root for*.

Figure 8.2 displays how often fans referred to those reasons or themes in their answers to the question about *what they currently like about the team*.

The two charts jointly establish a blended ordering of factors in the discussion that follows. I review and illustrate each category of response as it pertains to fans' original preference of a team to watch and follow, and what they like currently about being a fan (why they continue to like the team).

The role of family

Second only to "home team"/residential proximity in importance is the influence

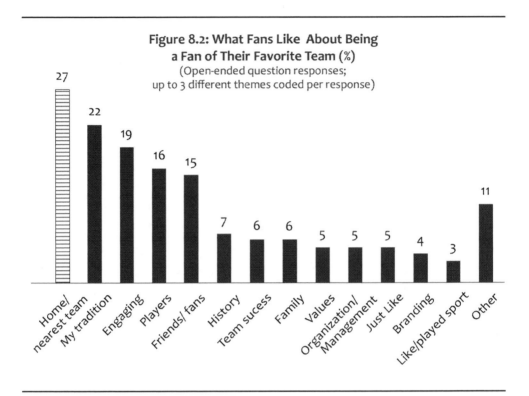

Figure 8.2: What Fans Like About Being
a Fan of Their Favorite Team (%)
(Open-ended question responses;
up to 3 different themes coded per response)

of **family** in sports fans' choice of a favorite team to root for. (Like some of the other factors to be discussed, because family itself might have been influenced by geographic proximity to team, the following discussion should not distract readers from the latter's overarching primacy to team attachments, as previously established. It is possible that in some, maybe many, cases these other factors indirectly reinforce its importance.)

Although existing research on the origins of team selection is scarce and quite dated, a 1996 study of college students found parents' interest in the team was the main reason for their selecting a favorite team.[128] Other studies, conducted in 1997 and 2002, obtained conflicting results, with geographic location and team success superseding family as the primary influencer. But even in those studies, family was consistently among the top several reasons for choosing a team.[129]

A number of responses from survey participants illustrate the influence of family in deciding whom to root for: A 50 year-old West Virginia woman wrote: *My father was a huge [Steelers] fan. I sat on his knee and watched the games.* A 37 year-old Tennessee man, a San Francisco 49ers partisan, answered: *My uncle was a big fan and I looked up to him.* A 51 year-old Alabama woman explained why she's a Bears fan: *They were my grandmother's favorite team.* A middle-aged Florida man said that he *chose the NY Rangers because my brother and my son got me hooked.* A young New Jersey male wrote that he became a Yankees fan *because my parents brought me to their games and I loved it.*

Table 8.2: Family Influence on Selection of a Favorite Team (%)	
Parent(s)	33
Spouse/partner	15
Sibling(s)	16
Family-other or unspecified	30
Family-net (any of the above)	**50**

Karen, a 30 year-old Pennsylvanian whom I spoke with, continues to root for the St. Louis (now Los Angeles) Rams, despite living nowhere close to either St. Louis or Los Angeles, because "the Rams remind me of my grandfather, who was a Rams fan." She began watching NFL football on television with her grandfather when she was a child.

Family was cited somewhat more often by fans describing a baseball team they picked as their favorite than by those who chose a football, basketball, or hockey team. This unique family-baseball connection is also apparent in what fans' *currently* like about their favorite team: Baseball fans are over twice as likely as those favoring a football, hockey, or basketball team to say they enjoy watching their team's games with family or sharing that sports interest with them. This might be partly because, as we learned earlier, those choosing a baseball team as their overall favorite are made up of a higher percentage of women than fans preferring other sports. It might also be that baseball games are more conducive to family outings because they can be less expensive to attend than NFL, NBA, or NHL games.

Fans could also mark which family members were influential in the original choice of a team to follow. Table 8.2 shows how many fans marked each respective relative as having contributed to their becoming a fan of their favorite team. Parents' influence contributed toward choosing the favorite team for one-third of all fans—generally the father, but not always. Siblings were influential for about one of every six fans (16%). Not shown in the table, for those who first became a fan of their chosen team at age 16 or younger, the incidence of parental influence rises to 50%; of sibling influence, to 21%; and that of any family member excluding spouses, to 66%.

It was not uncommon to mention cousins and uncles, and especially grandparents as having an impact on favorite team selection (included in Family-other or unspecified). For fans adopting a team as their favorite after adolescence, 15% indicated the influence of a spouse or partner—usually the husband influencing the wife, but not always.

Compared to the impact of family on fans' original favorite team selection, watching games or following the team with family members, sharing that common interest, or fostering family closeness is less often mentioned as something they like about being a fan now. Nevertheless, such answers describing what fans currently like about their team are not unusual. A young man from Vermont wrote: *My whole family are big Red Sox fans [so I am] too*. A middle-aged woman from Illinois described liking the Chicago Blackhawks because it's *something we can watch as a family*. A 40 year-old Virginia man explained why he likes the Indianapolis Colts: *They are my father's favorite team, so they are mine as well*.

Family-oriented responses are consistently more prevalent among female fans regardless of favorite sport.

Liking being a fan of my team because I've always been a fan ... Huh??

The impact of family also reveals itself in some fans' responses expressing that it's traditional for them to be a fan of team X—that they've always been a fan or have been for a very long time. More than a few such answers express nostalgic childhood memories of having watched their team, often involving parents or other family members. This theme is especially evident in responses from baseball fans.

Regardless whether the response includes a reference to family or not, what distinguishes answers classified in the **My (long) tradition** category is having liked that team as long as the fan can remember, as exemplified in the following answers: A 31 year-old male fan of the Chicago Cubs answered simply: *I've been a fan since childhood*. A 27 year-old male in Montana wrote: *I have been an Angels fan for as long as I can remember*. A 40 year-old Philadelphia Eagles fan from Delaware responded: *I've always been a fan—love Eagles football*.

Some readers might find such answers to be uninformative, only begging the question of *why* those fans have favored that team for so long. Nevertheless, it must be meaningful to those voicing that rationale, as it was the second most frequent type of response. This is what fans might be conveying, even if they don't, or can't, communicate it explicitly: Since I've been a fan for such a long time, it's become an integral part of my identity (so it must be satisfying or fulfilling), and thus it would be very hard, almost unimaginable, NOT to like the team.[130]

Appeal of the team's players

As a reason for initially choosing a favorite team or as a source of current attraction, fans often referred to the team's players, either individually by name or collectively. Most such answers refer to the players' athleticism or exciting game exploits, but others capture interest in players' off-the-field/court/ice activities and experiences. "Players" is the third most often expressed reason for fans' original attachment and the fourth most popular source of the team's current appeal.[131]

Liking or admiring the team's players is most common among fans whose favorite team plays in the NBA, perhaps because on a 5-man basketball team, impressive individual performances stand out more and are more common than in the three other sports. It could also be due, in part, to the NBA's greater promotion of its marquee players. The same distinction emerged in the earlier discussion of fans' favorite sport.

In discussing the NBA's marketing strategy initiated in the 1980s and accelerated in the 1990s, Mandelbaum describes how David Stern implemented that strategy, capitalizing particularly on Michael Jordan's immense popularity. In contrast to football and baseball, where team is the brand, according to Mandelbaum basketball accommodates a different marketing strategy—making individual players the focus.[132]

The following are a sample of responses falling in the "players" category, not all of them from basketball fans:

> *Larry Bird was on the team.*
> – Kentucky female, 44, and Boston Celtics fan

> *I'm from the east coast, and I really did not know too much about the Lakers, until I came to LA. When I saw Kobe Bryant play I became an instant fan.*
> – African-American California male, 65

> *I find it interesting to follow what the individual players are doing, even if the team as a whole isn't doing well.*
> – Chicago White Sox fan, 77

> *I watched Cam Newton when he played for Auburn and I like watching him in the NFL.*
> – 53 year-old Alabama woman who roots for the
>   Carolina Panthers

> *The players seem to be real people with real lives and problems and not just sports celebrities.*
> – 60 year-old male fan of the Tampa Bay Lightning

In a few in-depth telephone interviews, I talked with fans who had gotten to know one or more players on a personal level. Gerald, a musician and music teacher— and fan of the Chicago Blackhawks— enthusiastically related how he became acquainted with former Blackhawks star center Stan Mikita in the course of giving saxophone lessons to his son. Jeronda, 45, related how she'd met and socialized with several Carolina Panthers when she

Basketball fans, like all sports fans, enjoy arguing over the greatest player of all time. In recent years, the debate has mostly centered on Michael Jordan vs. LeBron James. Based on one statistically elaborate measure, player efficiency rating, MJ wins, but only barely.[133]

was younger. She remains a Panthers fan even though she now lives in Georgia and her husband roots for the Atlanta Falcons. Having had a positive encounter with a player is a powerful reason for developing (or maintaining) an allegiance with that player's team.

Enjoyment derived from watching the team play

Being engaged by the team's play refers to a wide range of positive spectator reactions to viewing games including they're exciting, fun, strategic, fast-paced, intense, interesting, close or unpredictable, and other reactions (mostly emotional but sometimes cognitive) that facilitate psychological engagement. Also included in the **engaging** category are references to the team's distinctive expertise and types of plays at which they excel. Enjoyment derived from watching games is the third most frequently mentioned reason for liking being a fan of the team. Psychological engagement is less often cited as a motivation for initially becoming attached to the team.

It seems natural that a team's entertainment value should be prominent in sustaining fan interest, as enjoying or finding satisfaction in watching one's team play is almost by definition what it means to be a fan. Additional support for the importance of game-related engagement comes from the rush I get from watching being the single most often marked reason (by 60% of fans) in the list of 15 possible reasons presented for liking a team.[134]

As with the "Players" theme, responses categorized as reflecting "Engaging" are more common among basketball fans than among fans with an overall favorite in the NFL, NHL, or in MLB—both as a reason for their initial attachment to the team and a reason for currently liking being a fan.

Examples of fans' responses in the "Engaging" category include: *They [the Golden State Warriors] were exciting to watch* (African-American male in Illinois, 31); *The Pittsburgh Steelers embody the fighting and rough spirit of football* (20 year-old Hispanic male in California); A 70 year-old New York resident answered that he gets an *adrenalin rush* from watching Buffalo Bills football. A 54 year-old fan of the Cleveland Cavaliers wrote: *They have some of the best 3-point shooters.* A female fan of the Oakland Raiders proudly explained: *I chose them because they were crazy and aggressive. They played with reckless abandon. In their style of play, rules were made to be broken, and they broke just about all of them. They were intimidated by no one.*

The role of friends and the curious importance of the team's fans

Sharing a common identity with other fans or enjoying the social aspects of fanship (**Friends/Fans**) was the fifth most often expressed theme in fans' descriptions of what they like about being a fan. It was far less important in the initial selection of a team to watch and follow. This theme incorporates enjoying the atmosphere at the stadium, court, or rink; also the social activities related to watching/following the team, such as tailgating and other partying. Forty-five percent marked they like *Sharing something in common with friends.*

Almost as many (42%) marked *Being part of the broader community of the team's fans* as one of the reasons they like being a fan. Some of these unexpectedly common responses referring to other fans, rather than to personal friends, made it seem as though the respondent is identifying as much, if not more so, with the team's fans as with the team:

> *How huge their fan base is. When you watch TV . . . it's no big thing to see someone in the background wearing Pittsburgh gear, no matter where in the country they are.*
> – 27 year-old female Pittsburgh Steelers fan

> *Ain't no other fans like (Arizona) Cardinal fans . . . We love to get together and root for our team.*
> – 37 year-old Arizona male

> *Philly fans are wild 'n crazy. We're our own breed. I like watching the fans as well as the football players.*
> – 57 year-old New Jersey woman; fan of the Philadelphia Eagles

> *Fans are very loyal and enthusiastic. [They] care about the meaning of the game more than winning.*
> – Ohio woman, 43; fan of the Cincinnati Reds

Eric Simons cites the research of psychologist Marilynn Brewer to argue that identifying with a team's fans (as much or more than with the team) is not unusual—and that much of the conventional thinking about sports fanship mistakes identification with the team's fans for identification with the team. In her view, the driving force is often a felt connection the team's fans rather than the team itself.[135]

In unusual cases, identification with a team's fans can be negative and lead to an alternative allegiance. Mike, a middle-age security guard living in Florida who grew up in Trenton, New Jersey, described how he rejected selecting the Phillies to root for—the natural choice given where he lived—because he regarded Phillies fans as "nasty".

Some theorists have drawn upon a venerable sociological theory the decline of 'gemeinschaft' or small community (once the primary source of friendships and family ties).

> As a result, many are forced to satisfy their needs for sociability in less personal, less intimate, less private ways... Sports spectating has emerged as a [way for spectators to] come together not only to be entertained but to enrich their social psychological lives through the sociable, quasi-intimate relationships available.[136]

The following are examples of the somewhat less common tendency to be influenced by friends in initial selection of a favorite team:

A 34 year-old female Texas Rangers fan responded: *I started liking them because of a boyfriend … and really came to like them.* A 60 year-old New York woman described how she started pulling for the New York Mets: *I was a tomboy and all of my male friends were Mets fans.* A middle-aged New York woman described how she came to be a Bills fan: *Friends of mine were very much into supporting the Buffalo Bills. They would go to the games every week. It was exciting to be around them.* An Ohio man, a 52 year-old African-American, described the origin of his interest in the Cleveland Cavaliers: *As a little kid, all my friends loved the Cavs, and this is all we'd talk about while we'd were playing basketball on the playground.*

Analogous to what I noted above in the discussion of family, being influenced by friends and the social aspects of shared fanship are also more apparent among female sports fans than among males. This is consistent with the popular belief that family and friends are more central to the lives of many women.[137]

Team success

Recalling from Chapter 6 that a team's successes, especially its recent record of wins, playoff appearances, and championships, was a likely reason explaining many over- and under-achievement anomalies in national popularity, we turn to examine the relative importance of success more directly, from fans' survey responses.

Based solely on the incidence of mentions displayed in Figures 8.1 and 8.2, **team success** would seem to play a relatively minor role in fan attachments. The six percent who cite team success as a reason for choosing or liking their favorite team appears pretty slim. However, nearly one-third of the fans marked they *liked that the team was successful at the time they became fans,* and more than one-quarter marked they *feel better about themselves when the team is successful.*

I suspect even those numbers understate the role of success in inducing and sustaining fan attachments, although it is impossible to know for sure. For one thing, some followers are probably reluctant to admit this motivation, finding it unworthy or crass. I base this alleged reluctance on the sentiment critical of "fair weather fans" mentioned in more than a few written responses and on the surprising number expressing pride in loyally supporting their team "through thick and thin." Also, as just noted, the team's winning record or recent successes in important games was a plausible reason that proved useful in explaining many of the anomalies in the earlier macro analysis of teams' national popularity.

If we were to do a careful analysis of game attendance or audience ratings, I'd bet recent success would emerge as a major explanatory factor. It's almost intuitive that rooting for a winning team enhances the spectator experience and has to be considered a significant contributor to what one likes about being a fan.

These quotes illustrate the "team success" theme in respondents' explanations of why they chose their favorite team: *They [the Seattle Seahawks] started winning big games and becoming a feared team* (71 year-old Washington man); *They [the San Antonio Spurs] have won many championships* (30 year-old Hispanic female in California); *[It] probably really started [when] we had a consistent playoff contender team in 2006* (Louisiana man, 39, New Orleans Saints fan); *Three Stanley Cups during the last several years* (Illinois male, 53, fan of the Chicago Blackhawks); *The Twins won their second world series in 1991, when I was 11* (Minnesota woman, 35)

Liking one's favorite team because of its fabled history

Although not mentioned as a contributing factor in initially becoming a fan, seven percent reported currently liking their team because of its illustrious traditions and star performers of earlier years.

A California woman, 82, whose favorite team is the Yankees, wrote: *I was born in the Bronx, New York. I grew up walking distance from watching some of the greatest players to play this game.* A 44 year-old Ohio man answered: *The rich tradition of the [Detroit Red Wings] team. I have seen them hoist the Stanley Cup 4 times and have been in the playoffs for 25 straight years.* A 24 year-old California female Packers fan wrote: *Green Bay is a historic football team with a lot of culture... Lambeau Field is iconic and watching players do the Lambeau Leap is exciting and makes you want to be there.* A 40 year-old Arizona woman explained why she's a Bulls fan: *I grew up in Chicago when Michael Jordan played!*

Liking one's team because of the values of the organization or its players

The **values** source of attraction includes responses such as doing good things for the community, participating in charitable events and activities, and in the team embodying positive characteristics such as diversity and tolerance. Also included are responses that the team treats fans well and the team's actions foster a broad sense of community transcending its dedicated fan base. "Values" answers could be referencing the team's players, coaches, or others in the organization.

Answers falling into the "Values" category are more important as a reason for liking the team than for originally choosing the team as one's favorite. Just over half (51%) marked *doing good things for the community* as a reason they currently like being a fan, and 37% marked they like *the values/behavior of the team's players, coaches, or owners.* Fewer (one-quarter) marked *doing good things for the community* as a reason they originally chose the team. That contrast could arise because it takes some time to become aware of the players' character traits and the good things the team does for the community; in other words, it would be less apparent before paying close attention to the team as one's favorite.

I suspect, in both cases—as a reason for choosing the team and for liking them now—those responses are to some degree, perhaps to a large degree, a form of rationalization to cast oneself in a positive light: If I've selected that team as my favorite to watch and follow, or if I like them now, they must have upstanding character and do good things. Otherwise, choosing them or liking them now could be cognitively dissonant. Many fans probably marked those reasons to acknowledge their team does participate in philanthropic activities and/or its representatives exhibit praiseworthy character. Nevertheless, because relatively few expressed those reasons in their written answers and because many who checked off those reasons probably did so casually and to rationalize their team choice, "values" is probably not a major factor influencing the fanship of many supporters.

Regardless of motive or importance, fans were fluent in expressing this orientation:

> *Players chosen are also people of good character . . .*
> *Arrogant behavior [is] not part of the Phoenix baseball scene.*
> – Male Arizona Diamondbacks fan, 69

> *I like how they donate tickets to military and vets.*
> – New Jersey Devils fan, 32 year-old woman

> *I like that some of the players are active in the community. They help out with many charity events.*
> – 30 year-old African-American woman in Florida, Orlando Magic fan

> *I like that they are not a team with a bunch of stars with big heads.*
> – Detroit Lions fan, 42 year-old woman from Michigan

> A 40 year-old hockey fan in Missouri was drawn to the Colorado Avalanche when he found out *they helped their local community more than any NHL team.*

Ethical values can also be a reason for *disliking* and rooting *against* a team. I asked Debbie, a 31 year-old Arizonan who follows the San Diego Chargers, if there is a football team she dislikes so much that she regularly roots for their opponent to win. She responded that she roots against "any team Michael Vick plays for." (Vick, now retired although rumored to be seeking a comeback, is the quarterback who was convicted of animal cruelty for participating in a dog-fighting ring in 2008-09 and spent 21 months in federal prison. He retired after played 13 seasons in the NFL for four teams.)

Liking the team's coaches, owners, management, or announcers

As in the case of perceived positive values, 5% and 2% reported liking their team and starting to follow their favorite team, respectively, because of **the style or strategies of the team's coaches, management, sportscasters, or owners:** *I like owner Dan Gilbert and trust him. I like the announcers, who are homers. I like the front office [too]* (56 year-old Ohio man; fan of the Cleveland Cavaliers). A 51 year-old New Hampshire woman likes the New England Patriots because: *The best coach is Belichick.* A 60 year-old female Michigander believes the Detroit Red Wings are ... *a well-run organization* *who are loyal to their players.* An African-American male living in Florida likes the New York Yankees because *they are willing to put up money for quality players.*

A Missouri man, 72, offered an extended nostalgic essay on why he became a St. Louis Cardinals baseball fan. His response is not fully reproduced here, but part of it is worth quoting:

> ...the man who made me a Cardinals fan for life was the greatest sports voice of them all, Harry Caray. I spent every game night of my youth and a lot of them after, my ear glued to the radio praying the Cardinals and Harry would bring home a winner. And if they did...."HOLY COW!"

(Caray went on to broadcast games briefly for the Oakland Athletics and Chicago White Sox before spending the last six years of his career calling games for the Cubs.)

A California man, 48, offered an affectionate, almost poetic account of the Dodger organization:

> I loved the O'Malleys, Walter Alston, Tommy Lasorda and, most of all, Vin Scully, who vividly described games that I could not see and provided the perfect soundtrack for those that I could.

Indeed, enjoying listening to the team's sportscasters on television or radio is a not insignificant source of enjoyment for many fans, as evidenced by the 51% who marked it as a reason why they like being a fan of their chosen team.

Branding

In contemplating all the possible factors that might attract fans to a team, elements of the team's marketing such as its **name, uniform, colors, mascot, logo, or promotions** would usually not be high on most lists. Nevertheless, the Sports Fan Survey found branding to be more influential than anticipated. Three percent of fans volunteered such elements in their response to why they originally selected their team, while four percent cited them as part of what they like about team. Over one-third (35%) checked off that reason as contributing to their originally becoming attached. Here are some examples of this theme in fans' own words:

> I just liked their colors, and their team name.
>   – 49ers fan in South Carolina, 18 year-old Hispanic male

> Pues su manera de jugar y el diseño de las camisetas.
> (The way they play and the design of their jerseys.)
>   – 34 year-old male Arizona Cardinals fan in Ohio

I enjoy receiving free items, and I remember the first time that I filled out for a free fan pack giveaway for the Denver Broncos, I was so excited and I thought the offer was something cool to have, and that the team was so kind to give this out and I have been following them ever since.
— 34 year-old African-American woman in Georgia

I like panthers.
— 30 year-old Virginia female, Carolina Panthers fan

I love the cheerleaders.
— 44 year-old male Dallas Cowboys fan

Liking/selecting a team because of liking or having played that sport

Some fans replied liking their favorite team because they **like that sport**, sometimes because they **play (or used to play) that sport**. A fan might like the Detroit Tigers, for example, because he/she likes baseball or because of having played baseball or softball. Such answers do not address why those fans chose or like their particular team, but it helps explain why they are fans.

A 59 year-old female fan of the Baltimore Orioles wrote: *I just love baseball. After all, it is a game of strategy.* An elderly Massachusetts woman and Red Sox fan likes that *baseball is a peaceful and slow sport.* A 40 year-old New York woman is a Buffalo Sabres fan because *I love the sport and support my city.* A Baltimore Ravens fan began rooting for the Ravens ... *because I identified with football.*

As many as one-quarter of big4 sports fans fall into this category, based on the percentage who agreed with the statement: *Because I enjoyed watching that sport, I could have become a fan of almost any team.*

Choosing a favorite team because of a memorable game or accessibility

Completing the list of factors in Table 8.1 are having originally chosen a team (1) because of an influential game the fan watched (sometimes the fan's very first game), and (2) because of easy accessibility.

Four percent described becoming attached to the team as a result of **watching them play first or because of some other memorable game** they witnessed. An 18 year-old New Hampshire female wrote: *My dad has been a Patriots fan his whole life and has season tickets so he brought me to one game when I was 4 and I've been hooked ever since.* A 41 year-old New York man related: *The first Mets game I ever saw on TV, Dwight Gooden was pitching, he just blew me away and I've been a diehard fan ever since.* A 40 year-old Louisiana man answered: *I remember watching a [Miami Dolphins]* *game with my dad and I rooted for them to win. And never stopped rooting for them.* A female Kansas City Royals fan responded: *It was the first ballgame I got to attend. The day was magical.*

Three percent said they became attached to their favorite team because they were easy to follow, because the games were available on television or radio, or because they played at an especially convenient location; in other words, because of their **accessibility.** As observed earlier, accessibility can be a reason for rooting for the home team or nearest team. But such responses don't always unambiguously reference the home team, or the main emphasis is on accessibility rather than support for the locals. As such, the category merits separate attention.

A 45 year-old Atlanta Braves fan in Louisiana explained: *I chose the Braves and the Cubs for the same reason—the superstations. I could watch both teams every day and I did and I still do. I love baseball and these were the teams that were available to me.* A 66 year-old Texas man described being able to get Houston Astros games on radio. A retired woman who roots for the San Francisco Giants said she chose the Giants because it was *easy to get to the ballpark.* A 61 year-old Pittsburgh Pirates fan explained: *I was a Mets fan for many years. They took off the Mets station from the TV lineup, so I started watching the Pirates because they seemed to be on every day.* A 29 year-old New York man wrote he became a Knicks fan because *the games were on TV most often.*

Strong local norms as a reason for choosing the home team; the uniqueness of New England sports fans

This theme reflects the sentiment of near inevitability about being a fan of the local team: That's what everyone does. It's almost unnatural *not* to be a fan. The norms are enforced by social pressures.[138] Only three percent cited **strong local norms** as a reason for choosing the local favorite, but those sentiments were especially poignant. For example, a 58 year-old female Steelers fan put it like this: *There was no other choice. I moved to Pittsburgh area and there was no other team that I could choose if I wanted to have friends.*

In other cases, being a fan of the local favorite was a milder norm rather than a commitment enforced by threat of social retribution. As an African-American Detroiter put it, explaining why he roots for the Lions: *Because this is where I grew up and everyone cheers for them.*

Might norms to support the local team be stronger in New England than elsewhere?

One fan of the Patriots wrote: *Just growing up in the Boston area, [it] was hard not to be a fan.* And from another fan of the New England Patriots: *They are the local team in Connecticut. Everyone is for them. Would be strange to support another team.*

In some cases, the threat can be greater than mere ostracism, as related by a 37 year-old Hispanic man in Massachusetts:

> *Well, in New England you either love the local team or everyone kicks the crap out of you, and I rather not have the crap kicked out of me. At age 7, I learned to love the game, love the sport, love the players, and love love love the Patriots.*

There is statistical evidence from the Sports Fan Survey to support the heightened intensity of New England sports fans. One item in the checklist of possible reasons presented asked fans if choosing the local team ... *was expected in the area where I lived when I became a fan.* Breaking out the responses by each of the nine geographic Census divisions indicates that fans in the 6-state New England area were the most likely to agree with the statement.

New England fans also stand out on another measure, displaying the largest proportion of high identifiers on the Sport Spectator Identification Scale (SSIS) introduced in Chapter 3, showing they identify more strongly with their favorite team than do fans in every other part of the country.[139]

Although I might not be the first to propose this explanation, maybe the characteristic has something to do with most New Englanders living in a semi-isolated block of states. If this line of reasoning is correct, then they might be affected by distinctively regional norms and traditions supporting strong sports loyalties. The intense attachments to their teams that we've uncovered among New Englanders might also be intensified by the fierce rivalries with teams outside the region, most famously the one between the Red Sox and the Yankees.

Two less commonly cited reasons for choosing or liking a big4 team

I couldn't conclude this inventory of reasons and motivations for choosing and liking a team without illustrating two additional themes—(1) **to be contrary or initiate a rivalry,** and (2) **to support an underdog.**

Some fans like to be contrary. They enjoy cheering on a rival or otherwise out-of-favor club to bait friends or family members. But the motivation isn't always pure provocation—wanting to give others a hard time. Sometimes atypical selections are made merely to provide a friendly competition or, less commonly, to balance a perceived imbalance:

> As one middle-aged woman put it: *I chose the [Oakland] Raiders as a way to stand out in a family of 49ers fans.*

> A Virginia man explained why he chose the Cowboys ... *simply because my brother picked the Steelers!*

> A young woman described the friendly rivalry with her father: *My dad was a Yankees fan but I was drawn to the Red Sox. To this day, my dad and I bet silly things on the games and it brings us together even if we don't agree.*

> A baseball fan in Southern California explained that he chose the Los Angeles Angels *[b]ecause the Dodgers got all the attention in town.*

Choosing a team to form a rivalry, regardless of how friendly, was a more common theme in the in-depth interviews. Richard, 36, lives in Arkansas. He and his two brothers have enjoyed following NBA basketball since they were kids. They decided early on that they would each select a different team to develop a competition to enliven their interest during the season. He chose the Boston Celtics; one brother selected the Lakers and the other picked the Bulls. Richard maintains his interest in the Celtics to this day.

Jean in California, 36, started watching football with her grandfather, a 49ers fan. Rather than "inheriting" her grandfather's interest in the 49ers, she chose instead to root for the Cowboys to set up an intra-family competition. As a Cowboys fan, she continues to enjoy a friendly rivalry with her friends, who mostly prefer California teams.

Finally, there will always be sports fans who sympathize with the underdog. Based on logic analogous to "effort justification", referred to Chapter 4 to explain why some fans persist in cheering on perennial losing teams, there is "greater potential return on the emotional investment in an underdog."[140] Whether or not rooting for the underdog reflects a tendency to project one's own psychological dynamics in identifying with disadvantaged contestants is an interesting question but outside the scope of the current analysis.

I must admit that "underdog-ism" is a powerful motivator for me personally. Other things being equal, I usually find myself pulling against the team favored by the odds-makers or for the one that's been down on their luck, as do the following fans:

> An African-American in Pennsylvania prefers the Philadelphia Eagles because ... *they are always considered to be underdogs against national favorites.*

> A Georgia senior likes the Atlanta Falcons *BECAUSE THEY HAVE BEEN UNDERDOGS!!!* (emphasis in the original).

A twenty-something Kansas woman said she chose the baseball Royals, among other reasons, because *they were underdogs.*

A Michigan woman listed several reasons why she likes the Detroit Lions: *Being from Michigan they are our home team. My dad, brother and grandfather watched the games together so it became family time. [Also,] they are the underdog, and I always love to see the underdog win.*

Summary

I earlier provided evidence supporting the conventional (and valid) belief that most fans—about three-quarters, according to the analysis in the previous chapter—pick the home team or nearest team as their favorite to watch and follow. The purpose of this chapter was to develop a comprehensive inventory of additional reasons for team attachments, assess their relative importance, and illustrate those reasons with examples in sports fans' own words. In many cases, these factors are not alternatives to proximity but supplementary, and in some instances they help explain the attraction of support for the hometown (or closest) team.

Table 8.3 (and Figure 8.3 in graphic form) summarize the main reasons identified in the research for selecting a favorite team. The relative importance ratings are based on a combination of the reasons expressed in fans' own words and the reasons marked in the checklists presented. I gave more weight to the reasons fans expressed in their own words because I regard them as a better measure of fans' true motivations. The relative importance of the factors is indicated in Figure 8.3 by the size of the shapes.

Table 8.3: Main Reasons Why Fans Chose Team As Their Favorite

Factor	Relative Importance
Residential proximity / home team	Very high
Influence of family members	High
Appeal of the team's players	Medium
Being emotionally or cognitively engaged by the team's play	Low-Medium
Shared fanship with friends and other fans	Low-Medium
The team's recent success	Low-Medium
Being influenced by a memorable game or series	Low
The team name, uniforms, mascot, or promotions ("branding")	Low

---

Figure 8.3: Why Fans Chose Team as Their Favorite

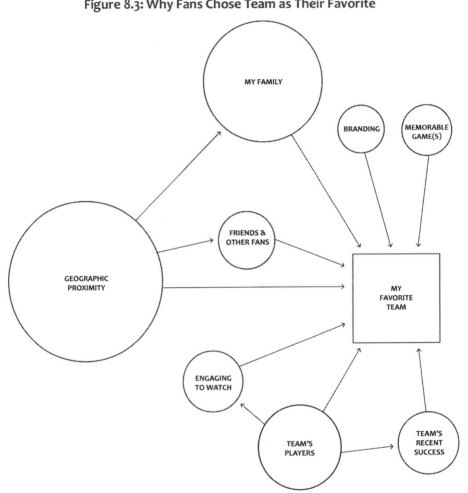

The arrows pointing from one factor to another (not to "my favorite team") are meant to suggest likely indirect influence

Table 8.4 (and Figure 8.4 in graphic form) summarize the primary reasons identified in the research accounting for why fans like their favorite team, more specifically, what they like about being a fan of that team. As with the reasons for initial team selection shown above, the relative importance ratings are again based on a combination of

Table 8.4: Main Reasons Why Fans Like Being a Fan of Their Favorite Team

Factor	Relative Importance
Residential proximity / home team	Very High
Having favored that team for a long time	High
Being emotionally or cognitively engaged by the team's play	High
Appeal of the team's players	Medium
Shared fanship with friends and other fans	Medium
The team's recent success	Low-Medium
Influence of family members	Low-Medium
The team's or its players' values	Low-Medium
The team's acclaimed history	Low-Medium
The team's organization or management	Low
The team name, uniforms, mascot, or promotions ("branding")	Low

the reasons expressed in fans' own words and the reasons marked in the checklists presented, with more weight given to the former. Also as in the previous diagram, the relative importance of the factors in Figure 8.4 is indicated by the size of the shapes, and the arrows pointing from one factor to another are meant to suggest likely indirect influence.

I end this chapter with a few comments on the principal reasons (beyond residential proximity) why fans choose a favorite team or continue to watch and follow that team. I also highlight a few interesting findings emerging from the analysis, apart from those primary motivations.

- Family members, most often the father but with many exceptions, are especially influential in fans' initial attachment to their favorite team. Mothers, grandparents, uncles, and other relatives are not infrequently mentioned. References to family in influencing one's initial team choice and as a source of enjoyment in sharing one's fanship are most common among baseball fans.

- A surprisingly large number of fans attest to liking their chosen team for no other reason than they've always liked that team or have liked the team for a very long time. It might be that some of these fans were just being evasive, not wanting to provide a more reflective answer. But many of them are probably conveying that being a fan of team X has become so solidly ingrained in their identity that it's inconceivable to *not* be a fan. There has to be something satisfying or fulfilling about it, but that something is difficult to articulate, possibly subconscious. This theme is observed disproportionately among fans whose favorite team plays baseball.

- Team success is probably understated in fans' responses as a source of team attachment because other evidence (as well as common sense) suggests winning must enhance the spectator experience.

- Compared to other fans, those whose favorite team plays NBA basketball are most inclined to be drawn to a team and its players because of the excitement and enjoyment they get from watching games.

- Sharing the fan experience with friends and with other fans is one of the most important reasons for enjoying being a fan of the team. The feeling of kinship with the team's community (the lure of tribalism?) reflects a desire for affiliation with those sharing one's team attachment. That turns out to be a surprisingly powerful motivator—and often underestimated.

- On most measures examined, female sports fans are consistently more driven in their team preferences and likes than are male fans by the influence of family and friends, and by the social benefits derived from sharing a sports-related interest with others.

- Less often mentioned motivations for choosing a favorite team (and/or liking being a fan) include the team's organization and management, the team's or its players' values, its branding (colors, uniform, logo, mascot, promotions), easy accessibility to watch and follow the team, simply liking the sport (in some cases, because of having played it), the team's glorious history, support for underdogs, to be contrary or initiate a rivalry, and strong social or civic norms.

- An incidental finding occasioned by the comments of several New Englanders (and reinforced by my own personal experience) suggests fans in that region are more passionate about their favorite team than are fans in other parts of the country. As both cause and consequence, social pressures to support the local favorite might be greater there than elsewhere.

I've identified a variety of reasons, some of them novel, why people become and remain attached to teams. As noted, most fans expressed or marked multiple causes to explain the origin of their attachment and the reasons that sustain their allegiance. The possibilities hardly conflict with one another and might in fact be mutually

Figure 8.4: Main Reasons Why Fans Like Being a Fan of Their Favorite Team

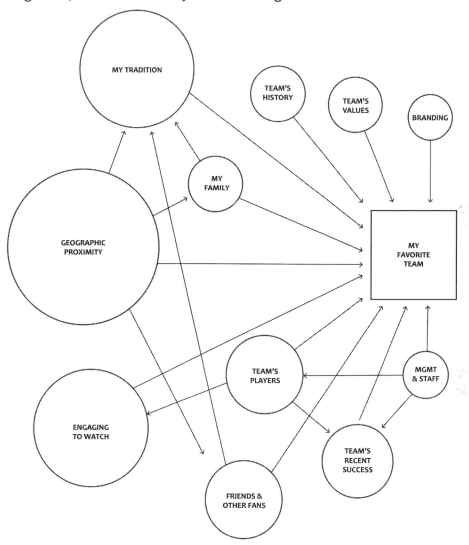

reinforcing.[141] A more detailed analysis examining multiple factors simultaneously is beyond the scope of this book. I leave that work to future researchers, who hopefully will build on the foundation laid here.

Chapter 9:

Switching Teams

I was an Orioles fan at first, but since moving to Pittsburgh I have become a fan of the Pirates' hard work and sportsmanship.
– Pennsylvania man, explaining why his allegiance shifted

In each of the previous two chapters, we examined what drives sports fans' team allegiances from complementary perspectives—how they originally came to choose a team to follow and what they currently like about being a fan. Before concluding, we take a look at shifting loyalties: How many fans change their primary allegiance from one team to another? Who are these fans? Do they differ from non-switchers in preferences or background characteristics? And perhaps most interestingly, why did they shift their allegiance? The data presented here is based on fans' overall favorite team—their number 1 across all the sports they follow—as in the previous two chapters.

Number of switchers and their characteristics

A mere one-quarter of fans in the Sports Fan Survey (25%) marked *they'd sometime in the past had a different favorite team (in the same sport) than their current favorite*. As someone who has had a series of shifting loyalties in my 6-decade tenure as a sports fan, I'd expected a larger number of fans to have switched.

Some fan segments are more likely than others to have changed their favorite team at some time in the past. Fans of an NBA team are most likely to have switched. Fans whose overall big4 favorite is a hockey team are least likely to have switched. Football and baseball fans fall in between. (Figure 9.1)

We earlier found that NHL fans are the most likely to cite residential proximity in explaining the reason for their team preference (both initially and currently), while NBA enthusiasts are the least likely to do so, suggesting, consistent with the data in Figure 9.1, that hockey fans are the most locally oriented in their team preferences, while basketball fans are the least locally oriented.

Another possible reason for the relative stability of hockey fans' loyalties comes to mind: When you subtract the seven Canadian teams, we're left with 23 teams located in the U.S. This compares with 32 football teams, 29 baseball teams, and 29 basketball teams. Although switching allegiances to or from a Canadian team is surely not out of

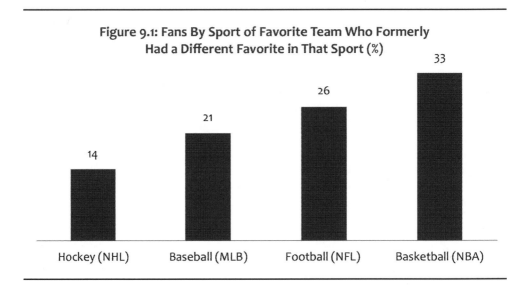

Figure 9.1: Fans By Sport of Favorite Team Who Formerly Had a Different Favorite in That Sport (%)

the question, it is statistically less likely. (Tables 6.2-6.4 confirm that it is uncommon for American fans to a root for Canadian teams.)

Prior analysis also indicated basketball fans are more driven by attraction to individual players than are fans of other sports. One basketball fan I spoke with (James, an African-American, retired and living in Florida) explained that his favorite team changes often, based on who the best players are at any time and which team is the best. This would seem to be an extreme example of frequent shifting loyalties, but similar views were offered by other basketball fans I spoke with—William (29) in Illinois and Paul (57) in Michigan.

If NBA players are most likely to change teams—purely hypothetical speculation, as I could find no statistics on the incidence of player movements between teams—then this could contribute to pro basketball fans being more likely than others to switch team allegiances. Or, it could be that NBA fans' team preferences are indeed more driven by which players in the league emerge as stellar or exciting performers, apart from having moved to new teams.

Aside from differences by sport, there are several other contrasts to note, mostly moderate in magnitude. Men are somewhat more likely than women to have switched favorites at some time in the past (29% vs. 21%). This could be because men are more

Table 9.1: Incidence of Changing Favorite Team
(Numbers in parentheses represent the number of fans in each segment)

When the fan lived closest to the current favorite team

	Only now (135)	Only when young (231)	Both now and when young (570)	Previously but not now or when young (47)	Never (298)
Yes- switched	57%	18%	17%	32%	31%
No- never switched	43%	82%	83%	68%	69%

avid sports fans, or maybe it's because men's identities are more bound up with the team they follow, as we learned earlier. When their team falters, according to this view, they would be more quick to substitute a new team to root for.

Regional differences are also apparent. Fans living in the Northeast part of the country (18%) and those in the Midwest (22%) are less likely to have shifted their favorite team allegiance, compared to those in the South (28%) and West (29%). I attribute this to the South and West having a greater number of new or relocated sports franchises.[142]

There is one additional contrast—perhaps the most interesting in terms of what we learn from it—in the tendency to have switched to a different favorite team. This one is based upon segments defined by whether and when the fan lived closer to their favorite team than to a competitor team. (This is the same set of groups analyzed earlier, in Chapter 7.) Table 9.1 presents the percent of each of these groups who report having changed to a new (current) favorite team at some point in the past.

The groups of fans *least likely* to have ever switched to a different favorite are those who lived closest to their current favorite when young. The group *most likely* to have shifted are those who live closest to their favorite only now. Those who have never lived closer to their current favorite than to a competitor team, and the small segment of fans who lived closest at some previous time but NOT when young or now, fall in between.

What does this mean? It suggests home team (or residentially nearest team) allegiances that develop when young are especially resistant to change. *The persistence of childhood/adolescent team attachments is underscored by the finding that those who*

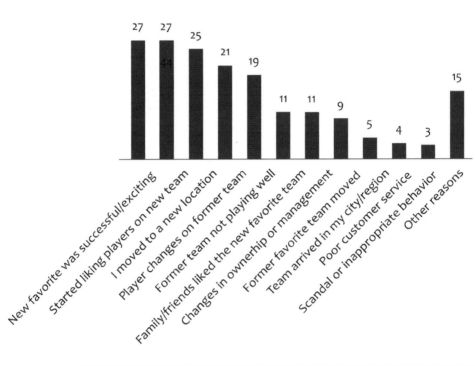

Figure 9.2: Reasons for Switching Away From Former Favorite to a New Favorite Team

lived closest to their current favorite only when they were young are as likely to still favor that team as those who have continued to live closest to their favorite team. (The 1-point difference between 17% and 18% is not statistically meaningful.)

In short, becoming attached to a local team when young produces a loyalty that tends to persist. This might be because those attachments likely have unique potency, not unlike other youthful emotional attachments.

Reasons for switching the team fans most like to watch and follow

Sports fans who had switched favorite teams were asked to mark the reasons they substituted their current favorite team for their former favorite. They could mark multiple reasons. The percentage of changers marking each of the reasons presented is shown in Figure 9.2:

The reasons fans marked to signal why they shifted allegiances represent a combination of factors that "pulled" them toward their new (current) favorite team and "pushed" them away from their former favorite. The two most common reasons, both pull factors marked by 27% of with switchers, are:

- My new favorite team was successful or exciting to watch.
- I started liking some players on my new favorite team.

The three next most often selected reasons for switching allegiances are:

- I moved to a new location (25%).
- My former team lost players I liked or acquired players I disliked (21%).
- My former favorite team was not successful or not playing well (19%).

Two of these are "push" factors, and the third ("I moved to a new location") doesn't fit neatly into either category.

Beyond those top five reasons, there is a sharp drop-off among the remaining listed reasons, none of which are marked by more than 11% of the switchers. To round out the review, about one in every nine switchers (11%) indicated being influenced by family or friends, and the same proportion cited changes in the team's ownership or management (which could apply to either the former or new favorite). Team relocation accounts for the next most often marked reasons—the former favorite moving away (9%) or the new team either moving to the fan's area or a new franchise being established there (5%). Still fewer switchers cited poor customer service or scandal or inappropriate behavior by the former favorite.

Summary

Only one out of every four big4 sports fans reports ever having had a different favorite team than the one they have now. Basketball fans are most likely to have switched teams at some time in the past; hockey fans are most likely to have stayed with the same favorite team. Male sports fans and those living in the South and West are also more likely than their counterparts to have switched favorites.

Fans whose current favorite team was their hometown (or nearest) team when they were young, including those who have since moved and now live closer to a different team in that sport, are most likely to hang onto that attachment. Other segments of fans, especially those who only now live closest to their favorite team, are more likely to have shifted allegiances at some time. These patterns provide strong support for the robustness of early local loyalties.

The most common reasons for switching favorites are:

- being attracted by the success or exciting play of their new favorite team,
- being attracted to players on the new favorite,
- having moved to a new location,
- player changes on the former team, and
- being disappointed with the play of their former team.

Chapter 10:

America's Sports Fans and Their Teams

I like pro football more than life itself because ... football provides more
thrills than life itself. And I feel the same way about pro basketball,
professional ice hockey, and major league baseball ... because they provide
an exhilaration that cannot be found anywhere else, and because they moor
me to my youth, my family, my friends, and the city of my birth.
  - Joe Queenan, *True Believers*

My curiosity about sports fandom that began as a boy growing up in Toledo has been largely satisfied. Why fans choose the Tigers rather than the Indians in Major League Baseball or the Lions over the Browns in pro football (if not also the Buckeyes over the Wolverines at the college level) can now be better understood by using the research presented here. Not that we can make consistently correct predictions about fans' attachments based on knowing a few facts about those fans—that would be an unrealistic expectation—but the foregoing should provide a better understanding of which sports and teams fans watch and follow. It should also help answer a couple of simpler questions: Who *are* America's sports fans, and what sports do they like?

Why fans follow sports and root for teams

Because a single survey can provide only a snapshot in time while the population is constantly changing, as are fans' collective preferences, the profile developed here might be quite different a year from now, and most probably different five years down the road. Nevertheless, the underlying motivations for fans' sports preferences and team allegiances are unlikely to change as fast. Yes, we found that residential proximity matters most, and three reasons were offered to explain why—easier accessibility to nearby teams and accompanying news coverage, positive and negative incentives in the social environment, and because we identify more with institutions that are close by and familiar.

But other factors also contribute as supplementary drivers or, in some cases, as the primary cause—the main ones being influence of family (especially early in life), being engaged by watching games and admired athletes perform, team success, and the social benefits from shared followership with friends, family, and other fans.

People like to watch sports because it engages them cognitively and especially emotionally, because they want to support their favorite team or the place where they live, because it's their long tradition, in order to share something with family, for social reasons, and for other, less commonly expressed considerations. Sports essayists have put forth more profound reasons why people like sports that were rarely articulated by respondents in the survey:

- Because it allows for safe emotional expression;

- Because of its authenticity amidst the widespread phoniness in today's society;

- Because of the special clarity of sports performance and outcomes.

Switching favorites

Three-quarters of sports fans report never having had a different favorite team in the same sport than their current overall favorite. Because my own favorite had changed several times, this number initially struck me as exceptionally high. But my personal circumstances might be atypical. I'd moved to different parts of the country several times since leaving Toledo as a teen. I didn't grow up in an area with a single, obvious "home team" choice, nor was I influenced in my sports preferences by mom or dad (who weren't sports fans) or by siblings (I had no brothers or sisters). My background is probably far from typical.

Fans who grew up near their current favorite team—meaning the team was located closer to where the fan lived when young than any competitor—are much more inclined than others are to have never switched allegiances. (They make up about 6 out of every 10 fans.) This highlights the robustness of early life allegiances.

A profile

Approximately three-quarters of us follow sports with varying degrees of attentiveness. The proportion is slightly higher if we count all sports (individual as well as team sports) at the college or professional levels, and a little lower if we count only fans of the four major U.S. professional team sports. Most fans follow multiple sports, almost half following four or more. With only a few exceptions, spectator interest peaks in early middle age, regardless of sport. For all sports in the survey, more men than women are fans, although this might not apply to some sports not asked about such as ice skating and women's basketball.

The research also identified several other demographic contrasts—some of them predictable, but also a few that surprised. While I expected African-Americans more than others to be drawn to basketball and less to baseball and hockey, I never would have predicted them to be more attracted to professional tennis than whites are—

presumably a response to the prominence of Venus and Serena Williams.

Regionally, we discovered that baseball is least popular in the South percentage-wise (though not in terms of the number of fans because the South has the largest population); college football is least popular in the Northeast, and hockey is least popular in the South. NBA basketball is most popular among fans living in the West.

The apparent uniqueness of New Englanders

Another regional finding reinforces my prior suspicion that fans in New England are more zealous about their regional favorites than are fans residing elsewhere in the country, possibly because of distinctive regional pride and stronger regional norms. Two independent measures underscore this conclusion: New Englanders perceive more social pressure to support their local favorites. Secondly, more of them are high scorers on the Sport Spectator Identification Scale, a measure of how strongly fans feel connected to teams they root for. Others too have observed the special fervor that fans especially in and around Boston feel for the Red Sox and other regional favorites.[143]

Sports and team popularity rankings

Professional (NFL) football is the leading spectator sport by far—as measured by the number of fans who watch and follow it or by the percentage of fans choosing pro football as their favorite sport. Ranked by the latter metric, Major League Baseball is the second most popular, trailing pro football by a wide margin; NBA basketball ranks third most liked, following by college football, NHL hockey, auto racing, and college basketball. Professional soccer, tennis, and golf are tied at the bottom, rounding out the list. Judged by the number of fans who follow each sport, the ranking is similar, the only notable difference being college basketball nosing out NHL hockey for 5th place.

The Sports Fan Survey indicated that the most popular teams nationally in each big4 sport are the Dallas Cowboys (football), the New York Yankees (baseball), the Los Angeles Lakers (basketball), and the Chicago Blackhawks (hockey). The list of overall favorite teams—fans' most preferred team across the big4 sports fans watch and follow—is dominated by NFL teams, led, in order, by the Dallas Cowboys, the New England Patriots, the Green Bay Packers, the Pittsburgh Steelers, and the Denver Broncos. The only non-football team making the top 10 is the New York Yankees.

Theories offering clues to why people like sports and follow teams

Several interrelated perspectives were introduced to help better understand what drives sports fans. One focuses on sports' parallels with religion—how both capture one's spirit and devotion, exhibit an abiding collection of beliefs and practices, employ a similar vocabulary, provide periods of comforting respite from the routine rigors of life, and induce faith in the future. Some observers perceive a connection between the decline in religious participation and the simultaneous growth in sports fandom.

A second emphasizes individuals' search for community as an important force propelling interest in sports spectating. This view stresses macro-level societal trends like the decline of traditional family life, rapid technological change, and the rise of the global economy—in addition to fraying attachments to church—as weakening the bonds connecting us to others, and views sharing interest in sports with friends and other fans as a way of restoring lost community. A form of tribalism, rooting with others for a favorite team can fill the human need for affiliation with a group sharing common beliefs, values, and practices. It can bring people together, including those from different backgrounds. (Think of essayist Joseph Epstein's working in the Deep South alongside others with whom he shared little else other than an interest in sports, referred to earlier.[144])

For those who identify with a team, the role of fan can be a major source of pride and can enhance self-esteem, especially when the team is favorably regarded by one's peers. When the status of one's team declines, this may lead to diminished attachment; when it increases, attachment can strengthen. Identity theory compares our felt team connection to an interpersonal relationship and helps explain certain types of behavior that make fans feel better about themselves.

Identification can also be negative—a strong antipathy toward certain teams. While not much discussed here, the desire to root for a disliked team to lose, as Joe Queenan,[145] Eric Simons,[146] and others have pointed out, can also be a powerful motivator. The Sports Fan Survey did not ask whether fans regularly root against disliked teams, but it *was* asked in the smaller set of follow-up in-depth telephone interviews. Most fans I spoke with DO regularly root against a disliked team—predictably, a rival of one's favorite team (Examples: Yankees vs. Red Sox, Warriors vs. Cavaliers, Saints vs. Falcons, Giants vs. Dodgers, Capitals vs. Penguins), but sometimes a non-opponent that is disliked simply because of their disproportionate riches (Yankees and Dodgers), their ownership (Cowboys and Redskins), their success (Steelers and Patriots), or their alleged dishonesty (Patriots).

We learn to regularly root against such rivals because, as Wertheim and Sommers note, "the failures of our enemies can be just as enjoyable as our own successes."[147]

Effort justification is a theory that's helpful in understanding why some diehard fans support perennial losing teams. According to effort justification, such fans persist in their loyalty with the expectation that when the time finally comes when their team enjoys a major success, the satisfaction experienced will be particularly joyful, more than justifying the long-time sacrifices endured (Think Cubs). Some continue to root for teams whose fortunes have turned sour to avoid being labeled "fair weather" or "bandwagon" fans or, in other cases, because they emphasize loyalty as a personal value or derive solace from sharing their team's woes with fellow fans.

Baseball fans are different.

We learned that fans whose favorite big4 sport is baseball differ from other fans in several key respects. Compared to fans of the other sports, they are less drawn to the game by the action on the field and relatively more attracted by their allegiance to team or place. In a sense, some like baseball because they like following a team that happens to play baseball. Yes, this might seem backwards, but that's the way many fans expressed their love of the game. It is as though the team and the sport are melded together in their minds more so than for other fans.

More than others, fans liking baseball the most explain their attraction as a long-term affair, often reaching back to childhood. Their early recollections of following baseball are often suffused with fond memories of sharing the experience with parents, grandparents, siblings, or young friends. For many, being a baseball fan is simply a long-maintained practice, the motives of which are difficult to express. Such sentiments are not unheard of from fans preferring a football, basketball, or hockey team as their overall favorite, but they are more prominent among baseball fans.

Accordingly, when fans were asked why they like their favorite team (or why they started following it), fans preferring a baseball team were more inclined to refer to the influence of family on establishing their initial attachment and, also, to enjoy watching games with family members. Again, in these responses: (1) baseball fans had the highest propensity to voice nostalgic early memories of the game and (2) were more inclined to say they like their team because they've *always* (or for a very long time) been a fan of the team—an ingrained tradition that would be unimaginable to break.

As much of the preceding has indicated, baseball has different qualities and attractions than the other team sports, which requires a different—some would say deeper—perceptiveness. Gilbert, a 58 year-old Hispanic who works as a petroleum industry consultant in Texas, used to coach baseball. He pointed out how "you learn more about baseball the older you get, and there are subtleties that escape most inexperienced fans." This helps explain why it takes longer for fans new to baseball to understand and appreciate the game—a point that should be especially resonant if you've ever taken someone to the ballpark from a different country where baseball isn't played.

One last, particularly intriguing finding seems to separate fans who like baseball the most from other fans: Paradoxically, they tend to identify slightly *less* with their favorite team. Deeper analysis determined this is likely due to baseball having proportionately more female fans and older fans, who tend to be less passionate about their favorite team, regardless of sport than are males and younger fans.

The future of fandom

The biggest change affecting sports fans today might be increased access from new technologies. Technological changes have resulted in more choices in how and when to watch games beyond the traditional way—watching the action live on television. Easier recording, Internet feeds, and other enhancements that facilitate time-shifting allow fans opportunities to watch at their convenience—not just in real time. Live streaming offers fans the option of watching the action and hearing the play-by-play on computers or on hand-held devices rather than only on TV or radio. The proliferation of websites, social media, blogs, networks devoted exclusively to general and specialty sports coverage, and other non-traditional sources makes it increasingly effortless to follow the reporting and commentary about favorite sports and teams.

Moreover, technological innovations now afford fans more opportunities for interactive participation, such as via online discussion groups, when before they were limited to being passive consumers. These innovations have also facilitated social connections via development of virtual communities. A lot has changed, and there's no reason to think sports fans won't continue to be positively impacted going forward.

As we examined how team choices are affected by where fans live, a contrast emerged between age groups in the incidence of selecting a non-proximate team as one's favorite. Up to the age of 60, fans of differing ages have about the same likelihood of picking the team closest to where they currently reside or formerly lived as their favorite to watch and follow. But fans 60 and older display a greater likelihood of doing so, suggesting that these older fans have stronger local loyalties.

I speculated that this could be due, at least partly, to older fans being less adept at, or less comfortable with, using new technologies that facilitate watching the games and following the news coverage of more distant teams.[148] To the extent that this narrative applies, we can expect fans will increasingly select non-local teams as their favorite, as these fans who are now under 60 become an increasingly larger percent of the population. If so, we may be witnessing the early stages of the nationalization (or "continentalization" if we include Canadian and possibly Mexican fans and teams) of sports spectating.

In closing, I want to revisit a second aspect of fandom—its societal impact. Sports rivalries can become heated at times, between fans as well as teams. In some cases, particularly after critical games, excessive exuberance can spill over into property destruction and personal violence. Such actions, always regrettable, rarely produce lasting antipathy.

One reason is that, in the end, most of us respect the rules of the game[149] and the way performance is measured. However contentious was the contest on the field, court, or ice, the outcome is virtually always accepted as legitimate, and we move on to the next game or season.

As renowned sportswriter Thomas Boswell points out, it is not always so in other forms of competition. Writing at the time of Donald Trump's inauguration as president, Boswell describes how Americans are divided and angry over politics and policy, but they tend to be civil and fairly sane, though passionate, about sports. In sports, they draw upon a vast array of statistics to support their views. The facts are rarely in dispute.[150]

Beyond a reliance on commonly accepted metrics, Boswell also attributes the difference to the absence of ideology in sports: "When we have a deep attachment to unprovable beliefs [as in politics], ideas and emotions get intertwined." In contrast, "sports may be so deeply realistic that they are inherently anti-ideological."[151]

Boswell's reasoning recalls Joseph Epstein's insights that we like sports not only because watching enables us to view athletic competition at the highest level of performance or because of its authenticity (both key "motivations) but also, importantly, because of its clarity.

Not to sound Pollyannaish, but the way I see it the positive contributions of fandom in building community and solidarity, especially among people of diverse backgrounds and differing points of view, far outweigh its being a source of social conflict and disunity among proponents of competing sides. An optimist might even say sports has serious potential to be an integrative, UNpolarizing force in these divided times. We can hope it is so.

Afterword

In the midst of doing the research for this book, but after my national survey had been completed, a light bulb went off in my head with an idea for conducting a mini test of team selections among others who grew up in Toledo, Ohio, as I had. I remembered that a friend in my high school graduating class had been compiling an email list of our fellow 1967 graduates, mainly for the purpose of organizing class reunions. Her list contained approximately 200 names and email addresses. I quickly built a short survey focusing on sport team preferences customized for people who lived in Toledo during their teenage years at the same time as I did. After obtaining her permission to use the list to contact our fellow classmates, I emailed them the link to the the online survey.

Although I received only 43 responses, the results are suggestive: (1) In baseball, most favored the Detroit Tigers over the Cleveland Indians by a wide margin back in our high school days; (2) Similarly in professional football—most preferred the Detroit Lions over the Cleveland Browns; (3) In the heated college rivalry between Ohio State and Michigan, my classmates preferred the Buckeyes by a ratio of 2 to 1 over the Wolverines.

These results reveal that proximity (and the attendant easier access) matters more than home state loyalty in professional sports, at least for this small "convenience sample" who lived in Toledo some 50 years ago. Perhaps this is largely because they could watch Detroit team games on TV and get sports news and commentary more readily about Detroit teams. For college sports, Michigan and Ohio State received roughly equal coverage in Toledo, and there was no difference I can recall in being able to watch those schools' games on TV. So, in that competition, home state loyalty won out. (Also more Toledoans attend or know students who attend OSU compared to the U of M.)

One last finding from this mini-survey was personally satisfying: In addition to asking my classmates whom they favored 50 years ago when we were in high school, I also asked whom they favor now. Unexpectedly but happily for this Michigan grad, the 2 to 1 preference for the Buckeyes had reversed, with a small majority of classmates now favoring the Wolverines! With age comes wisdom.

Appendix: Research Methods

The survey and questionnaire

The survey, conducted online, was completed by 1,303 sports fans from across the country who watch and follow at least one of the four main professional team sports at the highest level (National Football League, Major League Baseball, National Basketball Association, and National Hockey League)—the big4, as I refer to them. An additional 522 respondents were screened out of the main survey because they did not meet the qualifying condition for the bulk of the research—being a big4 sports fan.

The 522 who completed only the screening questions consisted of individuals who reported watching and following one or more other sports at the professional and/or college level but not any of the big4 (107) and people who watch and follow none— neither any big4 sport or any other sport at the professional and/or college level (415). Before being terminated from the survey, these 522 respondents were asked their gender, age, race/ethnicity, and state of residence. The 107 fans were also asked what sports they follow. These data were used to weight the sample and facilitate estimation of fan populations and other characteristics.

The full survey consisted of a maximum of 45 questions, which most respondents answered in less than 15 minutes. The data collection—conducted by SoapBox Sample, a division of ISA (Van Nuys, California)—was split into two parts: Approximately half of the online interviews were completed during a three-week period in the fall of 2015— September 26 – October 19. The other half were collected in the spring of 2016—April 7 - May 25. The survey was divided in this way to balance out possible seasonal effects in the way people think and talk about their spectator sports interests and practices.

The samples

The book is centered on presenting and analyzing data collected from two samples— (1) sports fans and (2) non-fans. The sports fans sample was divided into two subsamples—(1a) fans who watch and follow one of the four main professional team sports played in the U.S. and (1b) other sports fans. These segments are introduced and further delineated in Chapter 2.

The samples were selected from millions of adults 18 and older who had signed up to participate in surveys on various topics in return for modest rewards for their participation. Potential respondents were selected from SoapBox's own pre-recruited panel and from other companies' panels with whom they have ongoing relationships. The companies that recruit these panel members obtain their demographic

Table A.1: Characteristics of Final Sample of Big4 Sports Fans (N=1,303)

Quota group (unweighted n)	Unweighted %	Weighted %
18-24 male (90)	6.9	6.9
25-44 male (279)	21.4	21.0
45-64 male (238)	18.3	18.4
65+ male (119)	9.1	9.1
18-24 female (66)	5.1	5.4
25-44 female (207)	15.9	16.0
45-64 female (201)	15.4	15.7
65+ female (103)	7.9	7.6
Total	100%	100%
New England (58)	4.5	4.5
Middle Atlantic (177)	13.6	13.7
South Atlantic (260)	20.0	19.8
East South Central (65)	5.0	5.2
West South Central (143)	11.0	10.8
East North Central (196)	15.0	15.0
West North Central (84)	6.4	6.6
Mountain (97)	7.4	7.4
Pacific (222)	17.0	17.0
Total	100%	100%
African-American (198)	15.2	15.0
All other races (1105)	84.8	85.0
Total	100%	100%

characteristics when they sign up to participate. For a researcher wishing to draw respondents for a survey from this pool of panel members, this facilitates obtaining a sample with the desired composition.[152]

Demographic quotas were established in the Sports Fan Survey so the final samples of fans and non-fans would be representative of their respective adult population with respect to age by gender, and by where they live (by the nine U.S. Census Divisions, which cover the 50 states plus the District of Columbia). A separate quota was also set to guarantee that African-Americans are proportionately represented.[153]

Because there were no independent estimates of the number of sports fans, as defined, in the U.S. population (combined with the intent of oversampling sports fans), we had no way of establishing accurate quotas in advance. We set initial quotas based on U.S. Census Bureau estimates of the adult population (over-sampling males with the expectation that males are more likely than females to be sports fans) and then adjusted the quotas twice—at the halfway point of the data collection and then again, with updated targets, when three-quarters of the survey was completed. Sample was released systematically throughout the data collection in an effort to fill the quotas evenly.

The underlying logic of this approach is as follows: The best estimates of the gender, age, and geographic location distributions of sports fans (as well as non-fans) would be known only at the end of the survey. But, as more and more information on those characteristics becomes available during the survey, we could take advantage of this fresh data by approximating the "true" sports fan population—and, most importantly, efficiently accomplish the objective of oversampling fans—through iterative mid-survey quota adjustments. Although this procedure would not guarantee a perfectly demographically representative sample, it would greatly reduce the need for large post-survey weights and their inflationary impact on estimated sampling error.

As shown in tables A.1 and A.2 displaying the final distributions, the data collection consisted of 19 sample quotas in all—eight age-by-gender groups, nine geographic Census Divisions, and two racial categories.

Weighting[154]

Table A.1 displays the final unweighted and weighted proportions of big4 sports fans in each of the quota categories. Comparing the numbers in the unweighted and weighted columns shows the effect of the weighting to be minimal and that the iterative quota adjustment procedure was effective in achieving its objective.

As noted above, the objective of the total survey sample (big4 sports fans plus other sports fans plus non-fans) was to be demographically representative of the 18 and older U.S. adult population. Table A.2 displays the weighted and unweighted numbers by quota group for the total sample:

As in the case of the sports fan sample, the unweighted and weighted percentages in Table A.2 are very close, indicating again that only modest-size weights had to be applied.

Quality control procedures

Unlike in surveys conducted by telephone or in person, where a live interviewer

Table A.2: Characteristics of Total Survey Sample (N = 1,825)

Quota group (unweighted n)	Weighted %	Weighted (Weighted to 2015 U.S. population)
18-24 male (121)	6.6	6.6
25-44 male (320)	17.5	17.2
45-64 male (302)	16.5	16.6
65+ male (151)	8.3	8.3
18-24 female (107)	5.9	6.3
25-44 female (309)	16.9	17.0
45-64 female (314)	17.2	17.4
65+ female (201)	11.0	10.6
Total	100%	100%
New England (86)	4.7	4.7
Middle Atlantic (241)	13.2	13.3
South Atlantic (366)	20.1	19.8
East South Central (105)	5.8	5.9
West South Central (143)	11.7	11.6
East North Central (270)	14.8	14.7
West North Central (116)	6.4	6.5
Mountain (129)	7.1	7.1
Pacific (297)	16.3	16.3
Total	100%	100%
African-American (259)	14.2	13.9
All other races (1,566)	85.8	86.1
Total	100%	100%

administers the questions and records the answers, online interviews offer little control over the care and attentiveness of the respondent's answers. To address this potential data quality hazard, I reviewed and "scored" the pattern of responses of each respondent's completed survey on an ongoing basis while the survey was in progress. Each case found to be substandard was rejected and replaced by a new respondent. The quota counts were updated accordingly.

These data quality reviews consisted of checking for missing or insufficiently complete answers, gibberish answers to open-ended questions, illogical and inconsistent response patterns, implausible answers, "straight lining" (giving the same response to a series of similarly scaled items), and rushing through the survey markedly faster than average (each respondent was automatically timed from first click through submission of his/her answers).

If a respondent's cumulative score on these criteria exceeded a threshold value, their data record (full set of responses) was rejected. One hundred forty-six of the records in the survey (11% of the final sample of sports fans) were deleted due to inadequate quality and replaced with new respondents whose responses met the quality threshold. These reviews, although time-consuming and labor intensive, were important in improving the quality of the data.

Follow-up telephone interviews

I personally interviewed 80 sports fans from the online survey sample who were selected from the much larger number who had volunteered to discuss their spectator sports interests in a more in-depth interview by telephone. As in the survey, about half were interviewed in the fall and half in the spring. The purpose of these supplemental interviews was to obtain more in-depth, qualitative information to add color and provide deeper real-life examples of the statistical patterns detected in the survey analysis. Collectively, the interviewees were chosen to reflect the diversity of sports fans' demographics, favorite sports, and teams.

Bibliography

Barber, Nigel. "Is Sport a Religion?" *Psychology Today*, 11 Nov. 2009,
    http://www.psychologytoday.com/blog/the-human-beast/200911/is-sport-religion.

Baseball Almanac.com. "George Carlin on Baseball and Football."
    www.baseball-almanac.com/humor7.shtml.

Berkon, Ben. "Why Fans Stand by Perennial Losers." *New York Times*, 31 Dec. 2015,
www.nytimes.com/2016/01/01/sports/baseball/why-fans-stand-by-perennial-losers.
html?smprod=nytcore-ipad&smid=nytcore-ipad-share&_r=0.

Bollom, Bill. "Future Popularity of Football Not a Sure Thing." the northwestern.com,
    Gannett, 2 Aug. 2015, www.thenorthwestern.com/story/opinion/columnists/2015/08/01/
    future-popularity-football-sure-thing/30984611/.

Boswell, Thomas. "In Sports, Rules and Results Matter. That's Increasingly Refreshing."
    Washington Post, 20 Jan. 2017, www.washingtonpost.com/sports/in-sports-rules-and-
    results-matter-there-might-be-something-to-that/2017/01/18/aad0f980-ddad-11e6-918c-
    99ede3c8cafa_story.html?utm_term=.981340e96f34.

Boudway, Ira. "Fixing Baseball's Old-People Problem." Bloomberg.com,
    2 Apr. 2014, www.bloomberg.com/news/articles/2014-04-01/fixing-baseballs-old-people-
    problem-with-merchandise-highlights.

Carlin, George. *Brain Droppings*. New York, Hyperion, 1997.

Chalabi, Mona. "Three Leagues, 92 Teams And One Black Principal Owner."
    fivethirtyeight.com, 28 Apr. 2014, fivethirtyeight.com/datalab/diversity-in-the-nba-the-
    nfl-and-mlb/.

Chandon, Peter and Yann Carnil. "When Your Football Team Wins, You Eat Healthier Food,"
    Washington Post, Outlook section, 7 Feb. 2016; https://www.washingtonpost.com/
    opinions/when-your-football-team-wins-you-eat-healthier-food/2016/02/05/40c17fd8-
    cb57-11e5-a7b2-5a2f824b02c9_story.html?utm_term=.7079a6b16a25.

Chase, Chris. "The NFL's Winningest Teams Over the Past 10 Years: RANKED!"
    USA Today, 12 Aug. 2015, ftw.usatoday.com/2015/08/nfl-best-teams-
    most-wins-playoff-appearances-super-bowls-new-england-indianapolis-pittsburgh-
    which-nfl-team-is-best.

Dietz-Uhler, Beth and Jason R. Lanter. "The Consequences of Sports Fan Identification." *Sports Mania: Essays on Fandom and the Media in the 21st Century*, edited by Lawrence W. Hugenberg et al., Jefferson NC, McFarland & Company, 2008, pp. 103-12.

Dunning, Eric. "The Sociology of Sport in Europe and the United States: Critical Perspectives from an 'Elisian' Perspective." *Sport and Social Theory*, edited by C. R. Rees and A. W. Miracle, Champaign IL, Human Kinetics, 1986, pp. 29-56.

End, C. M., B. Dietz-Uhler, E. A. Harrick and I. Jacquemotte, "Identifying with Winners: A Reexamination of Sport Fans' Tendency to BIRG." *Journal of Applied Social Psychology*, Vol. 32 (2002), pp. 1017-1030.

Epstein, Joseph. *Masters of the Games: Essays and Stories on Sport*. Lanham, MD; Roman & Littlefield, 2015.

FiveThirtyEight. "Which MLB Teams Overperform in Popularity?" April 1, 2014, https://fivethirtyeight.com/datalab/searching-for-the-most-popular-mlb-teams-relatively/.

Harris Poll. theharrispoll.com, "'Football's Doing the Touchdown Dance as America's Favorite Sport," 21 Jan. 2015,http://www.theharrispoll.com/sports/Footballs_Doing_The_Touchdown_Dance.html.

Gaines, Cork. "CHART: NFL And MLB Teams Top Premier League Clubs When It Comes to Making Money." BusinessInsider.com, 14 May 2014, www.businessinsider.com/chart-nfl-mlb-premier-league-revenue-2014-5.

Gantz, Walter, Brian Wilson, Hyangsun Lee, and David Fingerhut. "Exploring the Roots of Sports Fanship" in *Sports Mania: Essays on Fandom and the Media in the 21st Century*, edited by Lawrence W. Hugenberg et al., Jefferson NC, McFarland & Company, 2008, pp. 63-77.

Hugenberg, Lawrence W., Paul M. Haridakis, and Adam C. Earnheardt, editors. *Sports Mania: Essays On Fandom and the Media In the 21st Century*. Jefferson North Carolina, McFarland & Company, 2008.

Humphreys, Brad R., and Jane E. Ruseski. "Estimates of the Size of the Sports Industry in the United States." *EconPapers*, Örebro University School of Business, July 2008, web.holycross.edu/RePEc/spe/HumphreysRuseski_SportsIndustry.pdf.

Jacoby, Susan. "Baseball and Its Aging Fans." *Wall Street Journal*, 18 Aug. 2016, http://www.wsj.com/articles/baseball-and-its-aging-fans-1471534364?mod=itp&mod=djemITP_h.

Jenkins, Sally. "Amid the Specter of Terrorism, Our Games Become More Vital than Ever."
Washington Post, 20 Nov. 2015, https://www.washingtonpost.com/sports/colleges/amid-the-specter-of-terrorism-our-games-become-more-vital-than-ever/2015/11/19/bce291e0-8eeb-11e5-baf4-bdf37355da0c_story.html?utm_term=.10275a460367.

Jones, I. "A Further Examination of the Factors Influencing Current Identification with a
Sports Team. A Response to Wann et al (1996)." *Perceptual and Motor Skills*, Vol. 85 (1997), pp. 257-258.

Kang, J. Caspian. "Choosing a Baseball Team for My Baby Daughter." *New York Times*.
27 June 2017, https://www.nytimes.com/2017/06/27/magazine/picking-a-baseball-team-for-my-baby-daughter.html?smprod=nytcore-ipad&smid=nytcore-ipad-share.

Katz. Michael. "Chris Rock explains how Major League Baseball got so old and white."
SBNation, 22 Apr. 2015, www.sbnation.com/lookit/2015/4/22/8471165/chris-rock-hbo-baseball-video?_ga=1.255666376.1906780028.1469837876.

Lebowitz, Fran. "What I Don't Know." *New York Observer*. 4 March 2002, p. 15.

Lever, Janet. *Soccer Madness*. Chicago, U of Chicago Press, 1983.

Mandelbaum, Michael. *The Meaning of Sports: Why Americans Watch Baseball, Football, and
Basketball and What they See When They Do*. New York, Public Affairs (Perseus), 2004.

Melnick, Merrill J. "Searching for Sociability in the Stands: A Theory of Sports Spectating."
Journal of Sports Management, vol. 7, no. 1, 1993, pp. 44-60.

Minto, Rob. *Sports Geek: A Visual Tour of Myths, Debates, and Data*. New York,
Bloomsbury, 2016.

Monahan, Erin. "Why Is Football the Most Popular Sport in America?" LiveStrong.com,
15 Aug. 2015, www.livestrong.com/article/355384-why-is-football-the-most-popular-sport-in-america/.

Montville, Leigh. *Why Not Us? The 86-Year Journey of the Boston Red Sox Fans from
Unparalleled Suffering to the Promised Land of the 2004 World Series*. New York, Public Affairs, 2004.

Novak, Michael. *The Joy of Sports, Revised Edition: Endzones, Bases, Baskets, Balls, and the
Consecration of The American Spirit*. Lanham MD, Madison Books, 1994.

Pollack, Hannah. "The Dallas Cowboys Are Back on the Horse as America's Favorite Football Team." 22 Oct. 2015, *TheHarrisPoll.com*: http://www.theharrispoll.com/sports/Americas-Favorite-Football-Team-2015.html.

Powell, Jackie. "The Declining Number of Black Baseball Players Is a Huge Problem." overthemonster.com, *SB Nation*, 2 June 2016, http://www.overthemonster.com/2016/6/2/11806176/mlb-black-players-decline-red-sox-chuck-d.

Prebish, Charles. *Religion and Sport: The Meeting of Sacred and Profane*. Westport CT, Greenwood, 1993.

Putnam, Robert D. *Bowling Alone: The Collapse and Revival of American Community*. New York, Simon & Schuster, 2000.

Rovell, Darren. "Poll Shows Patriots Most Disliked NFL Team, Ahead of Cowboys." ESPN.com, 30 Jan. 2017, http://www.espn.com/nfl/story/_/id/18587291/poll-shows-new-england-patriots-most-disliked-team-nfl. January 30, 2017.

Queenan, Joe. *True Believers: The Tragic Inner Life of Sports Fans*. New York, Picador USA, 2003.

Scarinzi, Chip. *Diehards: Why Fans Care So Much About Sports*. Stockton KS, Rowe Publishing, 2015.

Serazio, Michael. "Just How Much Is Sports Fandom Like Religion." *The Atlantic*, 29 Jan. 2013, https://www.theatlantic.com/entertainment/archive/2013/01/just-how-much-is-sports-fandom-like-religion/272631/.

Shannon-Missal, Larry, editor. "Pro Football is Still America's Favorite Sport." Harris Poll, 26 Jan. 2016, http://www.theharrispoll.com/sports/Americas_Fav_Sport_2016.html.

Simons, Eric. "The Psychology of Why Sports Fans See Their Teams as Extensions of Themselves." *Washington Post*, 30 Jan. 2015, www.washingtonpost.com/opinions/the-psychology-of-why-sports-fans-see-their-teams-as-extensions-of-themselves/2015/01/30/521e0464-a816-11e4-a06b-9df2002b86a0_story.html.

___. *The Secret Lives of Sports Fans: The Science of Sports Obsession*. New York, Overlook Duckworth, 2013.

Sloan, Lloyd Reynolds and Debbie Van Camp, "Advances in Theories of Sports Fans' Motives: Fan Personal Motives and the Emotional Impacts of Games and Their Outcomes," in *Sports Mania: Essays on Fandom and the Media in the 21st Century*, edited by Lawrence W. Hugenberg et al., Jefferson NC, McFarland & Company, 2008, pp. 129-157.

Station Index. Stationindex.com, Broadcasting Information Guide, www.stationindex.com/tv/tv-markets.

Steinberg, Dan. "There is No Such Thing as Objective Truth. Just Look at Sidney Crosby's Concussion." DC Sports Blog. 2 May 2017, https://www.washingtonpost.com/news/dc-sports-bog/wp/2017/05/02/matt-niskanens-hit-on-sidney-crosby-is-the-ultimate-rorschach-cross-check/?utm_term=.9693681ff26a.

Tankersley, Jim, and Chico Harlon. "The City Where Your NFL Team Might Be Worth More." *Washington Post*, 11 Sept. 2016, p. G2; online: "We optimized the NFL by moving teams to new cities. Sorry, Cleveland." 8 Sept. 2016, https://www. washingtonpost.com/news/wonk/wp/2016/09/08/we-optimized-the-nfl-by-moving-teams-to-new-cities-sorry-cleveland/?utm_term=.c73be6c78c9d.

Theroux, Paul. *Deep South: Four Seasons on Back Roads*. New York, Houghton, 2015.

Thompson, Derek. "Which Sports Have the Whitest/Richest/Oldest Fans?" *The Atlantic*, 10 Feb. 2014, www.theatlantic.com/business/archive/2014/02/which-sports-have-the-whitest-richest-oldest-fans/283626/.

Wann, Daniel L., and Nyla R. Branscombe. "Die-Hard and Fair-Weather Fans: Effects of Identification on BIRGing and CORFing Tendencies." *Journal of Sport and Social Issues*, vol. 14, no. 2, 1990, pp. 103-17.

Wann, Daniel L., Merrill J. Melnick, Gordon W. Russell, and Dale G. Pease. *Sport Fans: The Psychology and Social Impact of Spectators*. New York, Routledge, 2001.

Wann, Daniel L., K.B. Tucker, and M.P. Schrader. "An Exploratory Examination of the Factors Influencing the Origination, Continuation, and Cessation of Identification with Sports Teams." *Perceptual and Motor Skills*, Vol. 82, 1996, pp. 995-1101.

Wertheim, L. Jon, and Sam Sommers. *This Is Your Brain on Sports: The Science of Underdogs, the Value of Rivalry, and What We Can Learn from the T-Shirt Cannon*. New York, Crown - a division of Penguin Random, 2016.

Wise, Justin. "Fandom, Company, and Conversation." The Cauldron, *Sports Illustrated*, 18 Dec. 2015, thecauldron.si.com/fandom-company-and-conversation-4be172d314f0#. gr5277j9p.

Notes

[1] Toledo is also the hometown of feminist writer and spokesperson Gloria Steinem and actor Jamie Farr—Corporal Klinger on the long-running TV hit "M*A*S*H".

[2] That store has since closed at that location and re-opened (under different ownership) in Maumee, Ohio, just south of Toledo.

[3] I led the team in hitting that year. In one of the most unexpected events in my life, I was briefly interviewed by a Baltimore Orioles scout, who was at the championship game mainly to watch the older players, whose games were to follow later in the day. My team ended up losing the game, finishing second in the city in our age bracket. I have only the fondest recollections of playing on the Stars for Gene Hoffman, our beloved coach , who was a detective officer for the Toledo Police Department.

[4] Of the 522 respondents who indicated not watching/following professional football, baseball, basketball, or hockey, 107 of them marked that they *are* fans of other sports at the professional or collegiate levels. They were asked which other sports they follow before they were thanked and terminated from the survey.

[5] One estimate, now dated, places the total dollars spent on sports spectating in the U.S. in 2005 at between $4.9 and $15.9 billion (Brad R. Humphries and Jane E. Ruseski, " Estimates of the Size of the Sports Industry in the United States," International/North American Association of Sports Economists, IASE/NAASE Working Paper Series, No. 08-11; (August, 2008). Estimated spending would be much higher a decade later.

[6] Chip Scarinzi, *Diehards: Why Fans Care So Much About Sports*. Rowe Publishing (Stockton, KS; 2015), p. 30.

[7] Quoted by Sally Jenkins, sportswriter for the *Washington Post* in her November 20, 2015 piece, "Amid the Specter of Terrorism, Our Games Become More Vital than Ever".

[8] Michael Mandelbaum, *The Meaning of Sports*. Public Affairs – a member of the Perseus Books Group (New York, 2004), p. 32.

[9] Scarinzi, p. 30.

[10] For a more detailed presentation of the societal impact of spectator sports that I've drawn upon, see Daniel Wann, M. J. Melnick, G. W. Russell, and D. G. Pease, Sport Fans: The Psychology and Social Impact of Spectators, Routledge (New York, 2001), Chapter 9, especially pp. 180-194.

[11] Joseph Epstein, *Masters of the Games: Essays and Stories on Sport*. Roman & Littlefield (Lanham MD, 2015), p. 10

[12] Joe Queenan, *True Believers: The Tragic Inner Life of Sports Fans*. Picador (New York, 2003), p. 206.

[13] "What I Don't Know," *The New York Observer*, March 4, 2002, p. 15; quoted in Mandelbaum, p. xiv.

[14] Described in Mandelbaum, p. xiv.

[15] Michael Novak, *The Joy of Sports*, revised edition; Madison Books (Lanham MD, 1994), p. xvii.

[16] See, for example, Walter Gantz, Brian Wilson, Hyangsun Lee and David Fingerhut, "Exploring the Roots of Sports Fanship," in Lawrence W. Hugenberg et al, *Sports Mania: Essays on Fandom and the Media in the 21st Century*, McFarland & Co. (Jefferson NC, 2008), pp. 63-77.

[17] Note that it's not necessary to be a fan of any particular team to qualify as a sports fan under either definition of "sports fan". However, and not surprisingly, virtually all who qualified as a sports fans in this research under the narrower definition did manifest a team allegiance. (Those qualifying as sports fans only under the broader definition were not asked if they have a favorite team.)

[18] Baseball attracts about 74 million regular season live spectators a year (in 81 home games/ team/year x 30 teams)—a figure that's been almost flat over the past 6 seasons. The NFL attracts approximately 17 million home game attendees (8 home games/team/year x 32 teams), a figure that's grown only slightly in recent years. The NBA and NHL (30 teams in each league) pull in about 21-22 million spectators/year in 81-game regular seasons. Attendance for pro basketball and hockey has increased modestly since 2010—a little more than baseball but a little less than football. (Source: ESPN)

[19] Estimates are from *Forbes*, cited online by Cork Gaines at *Business Insider*, "Chart: NFL and MLB Teams Top Premier League Clubs When It comes to Making Money," May 14, 2014; http://www.businessinsider.com/chart-nfl-mlb-premier-league-revenue-2014-5.

[20] Many other studies, although dated, support this predictable finding. See Daniel Wann et al, (2001), p. 9, for a list of sources.

[21] The survey question asked respondents to mark the racial/ethnic group that best describes them: White or Caucasian, Black or African-American, Asian, Hispanic/Latino/Spanish, American Indian or Alaska Native, Native Hawaiian or Pacific Islander, or Other or more than one group.

[22] Quoted in Eric Simons, *The Secret Lives of Sports Fans: The Science of Sports Obsession*. Overlook Duckworth (New York, 2013), pp. 213-14.

[23] The 107 fans who did not select any of the big4 sports as one they watch/follow were terminated from the survey at that point and not asked in the follow-up question to mark their favorite sport. Nonetheless, most of them listed only one sport. So, while the percentages might be slightly off, the rankings are accurate based on rounding to the nearest whole percent.

[24] Mandelbaum, p. 184.

[25] Rob Minto, *Sports Geeks :A Visual Tour of Myths, Debates, and Data*, Bloomsbury (New York, 2016), pp. 78-79. The college teams with the highest attendance are, in order: Michigan, Ohio State, Texas A&M, LSU, Alabama, Tennessee, Penn St., Georgia, Florida, Texas, Nebraska, Auburn, Oklahoma, Clemson, Notre Dame, South Carolina, Wisconsin, Southern Cal, Michigan St., Florida St., Arkansas, UCLA, Missouri, and Iowa.

[26] Nevertheless, later analysis (in Chapter 5) indicates hockey fans are even more inclined than those liking football the most to mention the rough, hard-hitting nature of the game as what appeals to them.

[27] This line of thinking is attributed to Michael Fitzgerald of the "Bleacher Report". Erin Monahan, "Why is Football the Most Popular Sport in America?" *LiveStrong.com*, August 15, 2015; http://www.livestrong.com/article/355384-why-is-football-the-most-popular-sport-in-america/.

[28] See, for example, Bill Bollom, "Future Popularity of Football Not a Sure thing," *thenorthwestern.com* (August 2, 2015); http://www.thenorthwestern.com/story/opinion/columnists/2015/08/01/ future-popularity-football-sure-thing/30984611/.

[29] Nor were there any other notable differences in *favorite sport* between men and women fans.

[30] Nielsen data also shows that the NBA has the youngest sports audience, with 45% of its viewers under 35, according to Derek Thompson, "Which Sports have the Whitest/Richest/ Oldest Fans?" *The Atlantic* online, Feb. 10, 2014: http://www.theatlantic.com/business/archive/2014/02/which-sports-have-the-whitest-richest-oldest-fans/283626/.

[31] See, for example, Ira Boudway, "Fixing Baseball's Old-People Problem," Bloomberg.com (April 2, 2014): online at: http://www.bloomberg.com/news/articles/2014-04-01/fixing-baseballs-old-people-problem-with-merchandise-highlights. See also Susan Jacoby's more recent *Wall Street Journal* essay: "Baseball and Its Aging Fans" (August 18, 2016); online at: http://www.wsj.com/articles/baseball-and-its-aging-fans-1471534364?mod=itp&mod=djemIT P_h; print edition Aug. 20. (WSJ subscription required.)

[32] Jacoby, op cit.

[33] Ibid.

[34] Minto, pp. 38-39.

[35] There are too few survey respondents in other racial/ethnic categories to permit reliable separate analysis.

[36] Jackie Powell, "The Declining Number of Black Baseball Players is a Huge Problem," SB Nation – Over the Monster, June 2, 2016; online: http://www.overthemonster. com/2016/6/2/11806176/mlb-black-players-decline-red-sox-chuck-d. The study was conducted by the Society of American Baseball Research (SABR).

[37] Michael Katz, "Chris Rock Explains how Major League Baseball Got So Old and White" (video) available at SBNation.com; http://www.sbnation.com/lookit/2015/4/22/8471165/chris-rock-hbo-baseball-video?_ga=1.255666376.1906780028.1469837876.

[38] Powell, op cit.

[39] This refers to the increasing emphasis on expensive training camps and personalized individual instruction for aspiring young players; also, the costs of playing on traveling teams.

[40] Canada's dominance of NHL hockey has declined since about 1970 in multiple ways—in the proportion of Canadians players, the success of Canada's teams, and fan interest. (*Minto*, pp. 148-149)

[41] In 2013, the percentage of blacks in the NBA was 76.3%--cited by Mona Chalabi in her "FiveThirtyEight" column (April 28, 2014); http://fivethirtyeight.com/datalab/diversity-in-the-nba-the-nfl-and-mlb/.

[42] The breakdown, by education level, is limited to big4 sports fans because the Sports Fan Survey terminated after a few opening questions for respondents who do not follow a team in the NFL, NBA, NHL, or MLB. Because only 107 of the 1,413 sports fans (less than 8%) identified in the survey reported not following one of the big4 sports, any patterns found here very likely apply to all fans as well.

[43] See Wann et al (2001), Table 1.2, p. 9 for a list of sources. Readers are cautioned that these studies are quite dated.

[44] One non-demographic characteristic asked about in the Sports Fan Survey is strongly associated with being a fan: For each of the four major professional team sports, and for men as for women, those who play the sport (or played when younger) are much more likely to be fans of that game.

[45] Michael Mandelbaum, p. 31. Identification with teams is discussed in greater depth in the next chapter.

[46] Scarinzi, p. 173.

[47] Most fans, but not all, selected their overall favorite team in their favorite sport (92%). Only they are included in the following analysis.

[48] Daniel Wann and Nyla R. Branscombe, "Sports Fans: Measuring Degree of Identification with Their Team," *International Journal of Sport Psychology*, Vol. 24 (1993), pp. 1-17. The full set of scale items are also presented in Wann, Melnick, Russell, and Pease (2001), p. 6.

[49] This might not apply to hockey fans, for whom the differences vanish. But the subsample of fans whose favorite team plays hockey (n=87) is small enough to remain uncertain about its generalizability.

[50] Readers should bear in mind that this analysis does NOT refer to all fans who watch and follow the respective sport; rather, it compares those whose *favorite team OVERALL* plays in the NFL, Major League Baseball, the NBA, or the NHL.

[51] Chip Scarinzi, *op cit*, p. 77.

[52] Quoted from Novak, *The Joy of Sports (1976)* in Wann, et al (2001), p. 200.

[53] Novak, p. 26.

[54] Ibid., p. 48.

[55] Ibid., p.30.

[56] Mandelbaum, p. 4.

[57] Nigel Barber, "Is Sport a Religion," *Psychology Today*, http://www.psychologytoday.com/blog/the-human-beast/200911/is-sport-religion, Nov., 2009. See also Michael Serazio's article in *The Atlantic* on the use of totems in sports—symbols of greater entities communities gather around for identity and unity— "Just How Much is Sports Fandom Like Religion," (January 29, 2013).

[58] Wann et al (2001), pp. 199-200.

[59] E. Dunning, "The Sociology of Sport in Europe and the United States," in C. R. Rees & A. W. Miracle (eds.), *Sport and Social Theory*; Human Kinetics (Champaign, IL, 1986), pp. 29-56.

[60] J. Lever, *Soccer Madness*, University of Chicago Press (Chicago, 1983). At the psychological level, Lever also believes spectator sports enable fans to transcend their existence and experience a type of spiritual transformation. Both of these sources are cited in Wann et al (2001), p. 200. See also Novak, especially chapter 2: "The Natural Religion".

[61] Wann et al (2001), p. 200.

[62] Gabriel Torres, sports anthropologist, quoted in Scarinzi op cit, p. 72.

[63] Most prominent in this genre of literature in recent times is Robert Putnam's *Bowling Alone*. Simon & Schuster (New York, 2000).

[64] Scarinzi, pp. 66-67.

[65] Lawrence W. Hugenberg , Paul M. Haridakis, and Adam C. Earnheardt, editors, *Sports Mania: Essays on Fandom and the Media in the 21st Century*. McFarland & Co., Inc. (Jefferson, NC; 2008), p. 9.

[66] Queenan, p.100.

[67] Dan Steinberg, "There is No Such Thing as Objective Truth. Just Look at Sidney Crosby's Concussion," D.C. Sports Blog (May 2, 2017); https://www.washingtonpost.com/news/dc-sports-bog/wp/2017/05/02/matt-niskanens-hit-on-sidney-crosby-is-the-ultimate-rorschach-cross-check/?utm_term=.9693681ff26a.

[68] For a broad-ranging review of sports fan identification, see Beth Dietz-Uhler and Jason R. Lanter. "The Consequences of Sports Fan Identification." *Sports Mania: Essays on Fandom and the Media in the 21st Century*, edited by Lawrence W. Hugenberg et al., Jefferson, NC, McFarland & Company, 2008, pp. 103-12.

[69] Wann et al (2001), p. 4.

[70] Ibid.

[71] Research has even found that fans' physical health can suffer when one's team loses. See Pierre Chandon and Yann Cornil, "When Your Football Team Wins, You Eat Healthier Food," Washington Post Outlook section (February 7, 2016), p. 4. https://www.washingtonpost.com/opinions/when-your-football-team-wins-you-eat-healthier-food/2016/02/05/40c17fd8-cb57-11e5-a7b2-5a2f824b02c9_story.html?utm_term=.7079a6b16a255a2f824b02c9_story.html?utm_term=.7079a6b16a25.

[72] Eric Simons, *The Secret Lives of Sports Fans*, Overlook Duckworth, Peter Mayer Publishers, Inc. (New York, 2013), pp. 130-134.

[73] Ibid., p. 131.

[74] Paul Theroux, *Deep South: Four Seasons on Back Roads*, Houghton (New York, 2015), p. 65.

[75] Ibid., p. 66.

[76] Ibid., pp. 66-67. Theroux attributes social identity theory to British psychologist Henri Tajfel.

[77] Eric Simons, "The Psychology of Why Sports Fans See Their Teams as Extensions of Themselves," *Washington Post* (January 30, 2015); online: https://www.washingtonpost.com/opinions/the-psychology-of-why-sports-fans-see-their-teams-as-extensions-of-themselves/2015/01/30/521e0464-a816-11e4-a06b-9df2002b86a0_story.html. For the physiologically arousing power of sports spectating, see also Scarinzi, *op cit*, p. 36.

[78] Lloyd R. Sloan and Debbie Van Camp, "Advances in Theories of Sports Fans' Motives: Fan Personal Motive sand the Emotional Impacts of Games and Their Outcomes," in Hugenberg et al, *Sports Mania: Essays On Fandom and the Media In the 21st Century*, McFarland & Co., Inc. (Jefferson, North Carolina; 2008), pp. 132-140. Another useful source, though a bit dated, is Daniel Wann et al (2001).

[79] Jon L. Wertheim and Sam Sommers, *This is Your Brain On Sports: The Science of Underdogs, The Value of Rivalry, and What We Can Learn From the T-Shirt Cannon*. Crown-a division of Penguin Random House (New York, 2016), p. 151.

[80] Ibid, p. 159. Wertheim and Sommers illustrate this with the recent success of the Golden State Warriors, and the unparalleled loyalty and enthusiasm of their supporters in Oakland's Oracle arena.

[81] Ben Berkon, "Why Fans Stand by Perennial Losers." NYTimes.com, www.nytimes.com/2016/01/01/sports/baseball/why-fans-stand-by-perennial-losers.html?smprod=nytcore-ipad&smid=nytcore-ipad-share&_r=0, (Dec. 31, 2015).

[82] Ibid.

[83] Daniel Wann et al (2001), p. 31 and passim.

[84] See especially the research compiled by and reported in Wann et al (2001).

[85] Baseball Almanac website: http://www.baseball-almanac.com/humor7.shtml. The sketch originally appeared in print in Carlin's Brain Droppings, Hyperion (New York, 1997).

[86] https://www.youtube.com/watch?v=aIkqNiBASfI. Many others have drawn parallels between football and war or military actions. See Mandelbaum p. 128, for example.

[87] Novak, *The Joy of Sports*, "Introduction: Faith Seeks Understanding," p. xx.

[88] Unlike the other survey data presented thus far, such "coding" decisions often involve inherently subjective judgments, as do the prior decisions about which categories to employ—why use of this type of "open-ended" question is known in research as qualitative

methodology. Not counting the 8% of respondents whose answers were either blank or indecipherable, the average number of codes given to the responses was 1.3.

[89] Because there is much subjectivity involved in classifying the responses, the percentages should be regarded as approximations rather than precise estimates of the proportion of fans expressing that theme. Modest differences, such as 45% vs. 50%, are not necessarily meaningful.

[90] Sixteen fans (out of 1,303 total) were excluded from this table because they gave inconsistent answers identifying their favorite big4 team.

[91] The answers quoted from respondents have been lightly edited for spelling, grammar, and typos, and some have been shortened to present the part of the response that illustrates the category highlighted in the chapter text. Readers are also reminded that some of the examples received other classifications as well as the one under which it is presented to represent.

[92] Daniel L. Wann et al (2001), p. 38.

[93] Quoted in Scarinzi, p. 186.

[94] Mandelbaum, p. 120. Interestingly, later in the same book Mandelbaum asserts that teamwork is more important to a team's success in basketball than in football or baseball (p. 205).

[95] While the Sports Fan Survey data cannot address this question with more precision, the relative importance of team and sport in accounting for spectator practices probably varies over one's lifetime and depends on the fan's unique circumstances in his spectating history. It seems plausible that many young children will initially be attracted to a sport by first becoming attached to a team, often via a parent's attachment.

[96] The two themes—tradition and family— were often conjoined in these answers, which posed coding difficulties. Should the answer be classified in the "My Tradition" category or in the "Family/Social" category? The solution adopted is based mainly on timing. When the response harkened back to and emphasized a much earlier period in the fan's life, the answer was classified as "My Tradition," despite references to family. When the response referred to family and pertained mainly to ongoing (current or recent) activities, it was coded as "Family/Social". Answers that pertained to both current/recent *and* long-ago times were given both codes.

[97] Mandelbaum, p. 52.

[98] Wann et al (2001), p. 46.

[99] Justin Wise, "Fandom, Company, and Conversation," *The Cauldron*, Sports Illustrated (December 18, 2015); thecauldron.si.com/fandom-company-and-conversation-4be172d314f0#.gr5277j9p Justin's father, Ron Wise, was one of my closest friends since our teenager years in Ohio.

[100] Mandelbaum, pp. 176-177.

[101] Epstein, p. 4.

[102] Some might surmise female fans are more value-oriented than males. They are only marginally more so, according to the Sports Fan Survey data—and not enough to feel confident that a true relationship exists.

[103] Queenan, p. 209.

[104] Scarinzi, p. 191-92.

[105] Epstein, p. 8.

[106] Ibid., p. 9.

[107] Unfortunately, there are not enough respondents of individual teams to break out those answers in Chapter 7 by team. They will be analyzed overall, by sport, and strong demographic patterns will also be noted.

[108] This seems to be a reasonable premise. For teams located in smaller markets, however, the fan base subsamples will be correspondingly smaller and, admittedly, their reliability won't be as good. The correspondence *won't* apply to the Canadian teams for obvious reasons.

[109] Adjustments need to be made in these calculations for teams in regions/markets with multiple teams in the same sport, for example, San Francisco/Oakland in baseball and football, where the markets are shared or overlap.

[110] The Harris Interactive online confirms the Cowboys were the nation's favorite NFL team as of early 2015: Hannah Pollack, "The Dallas Cowboys Are Back on the Horse as America's Favorite Football Team," *TheHarrisPoll.com*: http://www.theharrispoll.com/sports/Americas-Favorite-Football-Team-2015.html, (Oct. 22, 2015). One year later, in early 2016, the Cowboys had maintained their dominant position among fans according to Harris Poll editor Larry Shannon-Missal ("Pro Football is Still America's Favorite Sport," http://www.harrispollonline.com (Jan. 26, 2016).

[111] I use www.stationindex.com/tv/tv-markets as the source of the television market rankings in this chapter. (Media market size ranks are for 2015.)

[112] Chris Chase, *ForTheWin*, "The NFL's Winningest Teams Over the Past 10 Years: RANKED!" (August 12, 2015), http://ftw.usatoday.com/2015/08/nfl-best-teams-most-wins-playoff-appearances-super-bowls-new-england-indianapolis-pittsburgh-which-nfl-team-is-best.

[113] Some might wonder how the Packers could be the 4th most popular NFL team and the 3rd most popular team overall. This is how: The 75 Packer football fans had only 13 "defections" in answering which is their *overall* favorite big4 sports team, with 62 of them selecting the Packers as their overall favorite. The Denver Broncos, whom the Packers jumped ahead of in overall popularity, had 22 defections (from 78 who designated them their favorite football team), leaving 56 who selected the Broncos as their overall favorite. The Broncos also fell behind the Steelers in overall popularity, as the latter lost 12 fans to a different big4 sport: Of the 72 Steeler football fans, 60 chose the Steelers as their overall favorite team.

[114] See https://www.bing.com/images/search?q=NFL+Fan+Base+Map&FORM=IDMHDL.

[115] Jim Tankersley and Chico Harlan, "We optimized the NFL by moving teams to new cities. Sorry, Cleveland." 8 Sept. 2016, https://www.washingtonpost.com/news/wonk/wp/2016/09/08/we-optimized-the-nfl-by-moving-teams-to-new-cities-sorry-cleveland/?utm_term=.c73be6c78c9d. See also http://www.forbes.com/nfl-valuations/ - 596b97fb46cb.

[116] Public Policy Polling poll results, reported by Darren Rovell, ESPN.com, January 30, 2017; http://www.espn.com/nfl/story/_/id/18587291/poll-shows-new-england-patriots-most-disliked-team-nfl.

[117] To be more accurate, based on Facebook "likes," there are more Yankee fans than Red Sox fans in parts of southern and western Connecticut.

[118] "Which MLB Teams Overperform in Popularity?" *FiveThirtyEight* (April 1, 2014), https://fivethirtyeight.com/datalab/searching-for-the-most-popular-mlb-teams-relatively/.

[119] Although I thought this was an original idea, I learned I am not the first observer to propose this weather related explanation. Mandelbaum (pp. 288-89) also mentions it as one of three reasons New Englanders feel so connected to the Red Sox.

[120] FiveThirtyEight, "Which MLB Teams Overperform in Popularity?" op cit.

[121] The only player mentioned more often than James in those overall favorite responses was Peyton Manning, just retired from the Denver Broncos. In the *percentage* of fans of the team who mentioned a player, however, James is the clear leader.

[122] It's important to acknowledge the practical challenges faced in addressing this question. Sports fans are no different than other people in their inability to know what truly motivates them and, sometimes, also in their unwillingness to admit what drives their preferences and practices.

Using open-ended questions to elicit, without prompting, answers in respondents' own words is similar in approach to the approach used earlier (Chapter 5) to determine why fans like their favorite big4 *sport*. Likewise, the answers here have been classified into distinctive thematic categories, along with how many respondents gave each type of answer.

Recognizing that some answers from respondents about why they like being a fan and why they initially chose their favorite team will be inexact or incomplete, I supplemented both questions with a pre-established checklists of reasons why they might prefer their favorite team. The latter will be used in the analysis to validate the answers fans give in their own words and, as warranted, to modify the conclusions.

[123] In the overwhelming number of cases—92% of the time—the choice of overall favorite team is from the sport selected earlier in the survey as the individual's favorite professional team sport. At first glance, it might seem like the remaining eight percent are responding illogically. But they are not, since it's not inconsistent to have the strongest attachment to a team in a sport that isn't one's favorite sport, especially if the person likes two sports almost equally as much (or can't decide).

[124] This formulation is admittedly a bit oversimplified, as media market boundaries, which might be more determinative of "natural" fan allegiances, are not coterminous with shortest distance from the nearest team.

[125] In cities or metropolitan regions with multiple teams in the same pro sport, we have to assume the survey respondents took the question literally. For example, this approach assumes Chicago Cubs and Chicago White Sox fans would correctly account for the relative distance to the two local ballparks when answering—Wrigley Field (Cubs stadium) and Guaranteed Rate Field on the south side (White Sox stadium).

[126] The next most common type of answer, given by 26%, referred to the influence of family members on their team choice. While there's no way to know how many, some of those family members might too have been affected by residential proximity, thus conveying an indirect impact. Similarly for some of the other, less common responses ("friends/fans", "accessible"). So 41% might underestimate the impact of this measure.

[127] The verbatim answers presented to illustrate this and later themes focus on that singular theme and are not necessarily the respondent's entire response to the question.

[128] Daniel L. Wann, K. B. Tucker, and M. P. Schrader, "An Exploratory Examination of the Factors Influencing the Origination, Continuation, and Cessation of Identification with Sports Teams," *Perceptual and Motor Skills*, Vol. 82 (1996). The second greatest influence

was the talent and characteristics of the players. Residential proximity to the team and the influence of one's friends and peers tied as the third most prominent reason, and team success was only the fifth most commonly mentioned reason for originally identifying with the team.

[129] I. Jones, "A Further Examination of the Factors Influencing Current Identification with a Sports Team, a response to Wann et al (1996)", in *Perceptual and Motor Skills*, Vol. 85 (1997), pp. 257-258. C. M. End, B. Dietz-Uhler, E. A. Harrick & I. Jacquemotte, "Identifying with Winners: A Reexamination of Sport Fans' Tendency to BIRG," *Journal of Applied Social Psychology*, Vol. 32 (2002), pp. 1017-1030. Both sources are cited in Dietz-Uhler and Lanter.

[130] If this interpretation is correct, such answers suggest that the longer one favors a particular team, the more ingrained and resistant to change the attachment becomes.

[131] Further evidence of the importance of players: "I especially admired one of the players" was the second most often marked reasons in the list of 14 reasons for becoming a fan, and "watching one of the [team] players who is one of my very favorite players in all of sports" was the fifth most often marked items (from 15 reasons in that list).

[132] Mandelbaum, pp. 264-265.

[133] More details on this comparison are available in Rob Minto's Sports Geeks, pp. 132-133.

[134] Because it is admittedly difficult to thematically distinguish some of the responses classified as "Players" from those classified as "Engaging"—as both surely contribute to fan enjoyment—I've calculated a net figure—the number of fans whose answer was placed into one category or the other: For the question asking fans why they originally selected the team as their favorite, the net proportion is 19%. In contrast, for the question asking fans what they currently like about being a fan of their chosen team, nearly one-third (31%) expressed one or the other of those themes.

[135] Simons, p. 233.

[136] Merrill J. Melnick, "Searching for Sociability in the Stands: A Theory of Sports Spectating," *Journal of Sports Management*, Vol. 7, No. 1, 1993, pp. 44-60. See also Wann et al (2001), p. 188.

[137] There is no gender difference for liking being part of the broader community of the team's fans.

[138] Some readers might prefer this theme is better regarded as a sub-category of "home team / nearest team", which it clearly is. I treat it separately because, while it overlaps that category, it's somewhat distinctive and particularly interesting in its own right.

[139] I must note two qualifications to this finding: (1) The differences in mean SSIS between New England fans and fans in two other parts of the country (the East South Central and South Atlantic Census divisions) are small and not statistically significant; (2) Not all sports fans living in New England choose a local team (based in the Boston or New York metro areas) as their overall favorite, although more than 4 of every 5 of them do.

[140] Wertheim and Sommers, p. 54. The authors have more to say about why people pull for underdogs in the full chapter: "Why We Are All dog Lovers at Heart (but Not Deep in Our Hearts," pp. 43-58).

[141] It's also worth remembering that what we've learned about team attachments is based upon responses from fans about their *overall* favorite team—the team they most like to watch and follow. It's possible that the ordering of reasons for fans' attachments might be different if we'd asked the same questions about fans' favorites in the other professional team sports (not just their overall favorite).

[142] Also, older fans (over 45) are more likely than younger fans to have switched allegiances (32% vs. 19%), but that's probably because they have had a longer time (and more opportunities) to consider switching.

[143] See, for example, Leigh Montville, *Why Not Us? The 86-Year Journey of the Boston Red Sox Fans from Unparalleled Suffering to the Promised Land of the 2004 World Series* (New York: Public Affairs, 2004), cited in Mandelbaum, p. 287.

[144] Epstein, p. 10.

[145] Queenan, *True Believers*.

[146] Simons, *The Secret Lives of Sports Fans*.

[147] Wertheim and Sommers, p.194.

[148] Acknowledging that rooting for non-local teams is increasingly possible, one Virginia father wrote a letter to all 30 MLB teams asking why his newborn son should become a fan of their team. This fascinating story, In Daniel Steinberg's "D.C. Sports Blog" (June 17, 2017) including the replies he received, can be read at: https://www.washingtonpost.com/news/dc-sports-bog/wp/2017/06/16/how-to-choose-your-favorite-team-a-dad-asks-every-mlb-team-to-woo-his-son/?utm_term=.ce1c6d13fa58.

[149] Instances of cheating do occur among athletes—the main variety of late being illegal use of performance enhancing drugs. Use of PEDs has been a particular concern in baseball and in track and field events (including the Olympics). When discovered (or suspected),

it tends to receive major attention from the media—which is a measure of how seriously the public regards infractions. It has been a strong impediment for some baseball stars' election into the Hall of Fame, although attitudes on that matter might be starting to soften.

[150] Thomas Boswell, "In Sports, Rules and Results Matter. That's Increasingly Refreshing," Washington Post online: www.washingtonpost.com/sports/in-sports-rules-and-results-matter-there-might-be-something-to-that/2017/01/18/aad0f980-ddad-11e6-918c-99ede3c8cafa_story.html?utm_term=.981340e96f34 (January 20, 2017).

[151] Ibid.

[152] While there is an ongoing debate among survey researchers about the quality of pre-recruited panel samples, they are very widely used in marketing research and in many other tyzpes of surveys. Persons without internet access are obviously missing from the sample. However, it is estimated that 84% of American adults use the Internet (Pew Research Center, 2015). It is unknown whether the sports interests and preferences of adults in these households are different than others, but the disparities would have to be sizable for this omission to cause a substantial bias in the results. Since the survey was only available in English, persons unable to understand written English sufficiently were also unable to take the survey.

[153] We set the quota for African-American sports fans (big4 fans) to be 200, which equals 15.4% of the targeted sample of 1,300. The idea was to have at least that many cases to enable reasonably reliable inferences about the African-American population. We ended up with 198 African-Americans in the final sports fan sample, or 14.9% of sports fans in the final weighted sample. Of all 1,825 fans and non-fans participating in the survey 259 weighted (14.2%) and 253 unweighted (13.9%) were African-American. Another 27 respondents, 18 of whom are big4 fans, marked "Other or more than one group" as their racial/ethnic self-identification.

[154] The goal was to have a final total sample (fans plus non-fans) that is demographically representative of the U.S. adult (18+) population. The calculations required to establish the interim quotas and the post-survey weights were prepared by an experienced statistician with whom I've work closely with on previous surveys. Using 2015 estimates of the population and data from the survey, he employed a procedure known as marginal weighting (sometimes called "raking") to establish the data collection quotas and the post-survey weights.

Made in the USA
Columbia, SC
05 January 2018